BUILDING SCALABLE APPLICATIONS WITH MICROSERVICES ARCHITECTURE

Designing microservices for large-scale applications and understanding service communication.

NATHAN WESTWOOD

TABLE OF CONTENTS

ABOUT THE AUTHOR!

Dr. Nathan Westwood

Biography:

Dr. Nathan Westwood is a pioneering technologist known for his exceptional contributions to the fields of software development, cloud computing, and artificial intelligence. With a passion for innovation and a relentless drive to solve complex problems, Nathan has become a prominent figure in the tech industry, shaping the future of digital technology.

Born and raised in Silicon Valley, Nathan's interest in technology started at a young age. His fascination with computers and coding led him to pursue a degree in Computer Science from Stanford University, where he excelled academically and honed his skills in programming and software engineering. During his time at Stanford, Nathan was involved in several cutting-edge projects that sparked his interest in AI and cloud technologies.

After graduating, Nathan joined a leading tech firm where he played a key role in developing cloud-based solutions that revolutionized data storage and analytics. His work in the early stages of cloud computing set the foundation for modern infrastructure-as-a-service (IaaS) platforms, earning him recognition as one of the industry's emerging stars. As a lead engineer, Nathan was instrumental in launching products that have since become industry standards.

Nathan's entrepreneurial spirit led him to co-found his own tech startup focused on AI-driven automation tools for businesses. Under his leadership, the company rapidly gained traction, attracting both investors and clients who were eager to leverage his innovative AI solutions to streamline operations and improve efficiency. Nathan's commitment to pushing the boundaries of what's possible in tech quickly earned him a reputation as a visionary leader.

Known for his expertise in machine learning, Nathan has also worked with several large tech companies, advising on the integration of AI and data science into their operations. His work has spanned various sectors, including healthcare, finance, and manufacturing, where he has helped organizations harness the power of data and automation to achieve exponential growth.

Beyond his technical achievements, Nathan is a sought-after speaker at global tech conferences, where he shares his insights on the future of cloud computing, artificial intelligence, and the ethical challenges posed by emerging technologies. His thought leadership and commitment to ethical innovation have made him a respected voice in the tech community.

In addition to his professional accomplishments, Nathan is deeply passionate about mentoring the next generation of tech leaders. He regularly contributes to educational programs and initiatives designed to inspire young minds and equip them with the skills necessary to thrive in the ever-evolving tech landscape.

Nathan Westwood continues to be a trailblazer in the tech industry, shaping the future of technology with his innovative ideas, entrepreneurial spirit, and commitment to making a positive impact on the world.

INTRODUCTION: GETTING STARTED WITH MICROSERVICES

In today's fast-paced tech landscape, the need for scalable, flexible, and efficient software architecture has never been greater. Traditional monolithic application models, while functional, often fall short in the face of modern challenges such as rapid growth, evolving user demands, and the need for frequent updates and deployments. This is where **microservices architecture** comes into play.

Microservices architecture is a design approach where a large application is broken down into smaller, independent services that are loosely coupled but work together to form a fully functional application. Each of these services is designed to handle a specific business functionality and can operate independently from other services. The microservices architecture pattern is gaining traction because it enables teams to develop, deploy, and scale applications more efficiently and with higher flexibility.

What Are Microservices?

Microservices are an architectural style that structures an application as a collection of loosely coupled services, each of which runs independently. Unlike traditional monolithic architecture, where the application is built as a single unified entity, microservices decompose the application into smaller, more manageable units. These individual units—also known as services—are self-contained and typically interact with each other through well-defined APIs (Application Programming Interfaces) or other communication protocols such as messaging queues.

For example, in a traditional monolithic e-commerce platform, there would be one large codebase that handles everything: user authentication, product inventory, payment processing, order tracking, and so on. In a microservices-based approach, each of these functionalities could be implemented as a separate service. The user authentication service, inventory management service, payment gateway service, and order service, for example, would all operate independently, communicating with each other as needed but not dependent on each other's internal workings.

Each service in a microservices architecture is responsible for a specific business functionality, and developers can work on different parts of the system simultaneously without interfering with each other's work. Furthermore, microservices enable teams to deploy, scale, and update services independently, which is a key benefit for modern software development.

The Benefits of Microservices

The allure of microservices lies in their ability to solve problems faced by large-scale applications, especially those built using monolithic architectures. Let's explore some of the key benefits of adopting a microservices architecture:

1. **Scalability:** Microservices allow for more granular scaling. Instead of scaling an entire application (which may involve scaling unrelated components), developers can scale only the services that are under load. For instance, if your payment service experiences heavy traffic while other services are relatively idle, you can scale the payment service independently without affecting other services.

2. **Flexibility and Independence:** Since each microservice is isolated, it can be developed, deployed, and maintained independently of the others. Teams can work on separate services concurrently, making it easier to implement new features or updates without disrupting the entire system. This also means that services can be

written in different programming languages or use different technologies, based on what is best suited for the task.

3. **Resilience:** Microservices offer increased resilience. If one service goes down, the others can continue functioning. For example, if your product recommendation service experiences an issue, it doesn't necessarily bring down your entire e-commerce platform. This is particularly important in high-availability applications where uptime is critical.

4. **Faster Time to Market:** Microservices promote continuous integration and deployment (CI/CD) practices. Since each service is independent, teams can push updates to individual services without needing to redeploy the entire system. This means faster iterations, quicker releases, and the ability to deploy bug fixes and new features on demand.

5. **Optimized Resource Utilization:** By running each service in its own container (using technologies like Docker), you can ensure that each service only consumes the resources it needs. This is more efficient than monolithic systems, where resources are allocated to an entire application, even if only a small portion of it is in use.

Real-World Example: Monolithic vs. Microservices

To better understand the impact of microservices, let's compare a **monolithic** application with a **microservices** approach using an **e-commerce platform** as an example.

Monolithic Architecture

In a monolithic e-commerce platform, everything is tightly integrated into one single application. This might include:

- **User Authentication:** Handles logging in, signing up, and managing user credentials.

- **Product Management:** Manages product listings, inventory, and categories.

- **Order Management:** Handles the processing of customer orders, including payments, shipping, and status tracking.

- **Payment Processing:** Manages payment gateways, processing credit cards, and refunds.

These functions are all part of one large application. When a customer places an order, the monolithic system handles everything from verifying user credentials, checking product availability, processing the payment, and confirming the order. While this approach can work for small-scale applications, it becomes cumbersome as the application grows.

For instance, if the order management service becomes slow due to high traffic, the entire system—including user authentication and payment processing—can be affected. Similarly, updating the payment system might require deploying changes to the entire application, which could result in downtime or disruptions to other services.

Microservices Architecture

In a microservices-based e-commerce platform, the same functionality is broken down into smaller, more manageable services:

- **User Authentication Service:** Handles user registration and login.

- **Product Service:** Manages product details, stock, and pricing.

- **Order Service:** Handles order placement, tracking, and customer order history.

- **Payment Service:** Manages payment processing, including integration with third-party gateways.

Now, these services operate independently, each with its own database and API. If the payment service experiences high traffic, it can be scaled independently without affecting the other services. Similarly, if the product service needs to be updated, it can be done so without disrupting the user authentication or order management processes.

In this scenario, services can be deployed independently, scaled based on demand, and maintained by different teams who don't need to worry about each other's code. This makes the application more agile, resilient, and easier to manage.

What to Expect in This Book

This book is designed to guide you through every step of adopting and mastering microservices architecture. Whether you're just getting started or are looking to refine your existing skills, this guide provides the knowledge and hands-on experience to transform your understanding of modern software design.

Chapter Overview

In the chapters that follow, you will:

1. **Learn the Fundamentals of Microservices:** You'll begin with an in-depth understanding of what microservices are, how they differ from monolithic applications, and why they are becoming the

preferred architecture for modern software development.

2. **Get Hands-On with Microservice Design:** We'll walk you through designing scalable microservices that can operate independently and interact seamlessly with one another.

3. **Master Service Communication:** One of the most critical aspects of microservices is how services communicate. You'll learn about synchronous and asynchronous communication methods, APIs, message queues, and event-driven systems.

4. **Secure Your Microservices:** Security is paramount, especially when dealing with distributed systems. You will explore best practices for securing your services and ensuring that sensitive data remains protected.

5. **Dive into Orchestration and Scaling:** Learn how to orchestrate your microservices using containerization technologies like Docker and Kubernetes. You'll also explore strategies for scaling your services to meet growing demands.

6. **Understand Monitoring and Resilience:** Microservices require robust monitoring and failover mechanisms. We'll guide you through setting up logging, monitoring, and building fault-tolerant systems that can handle failures gracefully.

7. **Real-World Application Projects:** Throughout the book, we'll build a real-world e-commerce platform, showing how microservices come together to create a fully functional, scalable application. Each chapter will include step-by-step projects that allow you to apply the concepts learned immediately.

Actionable Insight: Why Microservices Matter

The shift to microservices can be transformative for your development team and organization. By breaking down an application into smaller, independent pieces, microservices provide the flexibility and scalability needed to thrive in today's tech-driven world. No longer will you be constrained by the limitations of monolithic architectures, where scaling and deploying new features can be slow and disruptive.

Instead, you'll have the power to build applications that can scale rapidly, adjust to user demands, and evolve without the friction and constraints of large, monolithic codebases. With microservices, the future of software development is modular, independent, and far more efficient.

In this book, we'll give you the tools and knowledge you need to start implementing microservices today. Whether you are building a new application or migrating an existing monolithic system to microservices, we'll walk you through the key steps to make your journey a success. By the end of this book, you'll have the skills to design, implement, and manage microservices that can power modern, scalable, and efficient applications.

CHAPTER 1: UNDERSTANDING MICROSERVICES ARCHITECTURE

Microservices architecture has become the de facto standard for designing large-scale, distributed applications. It represents a shift from traditional monolithic approaches, offering developers and organizations the flexibility to scale, deploy, and manage applications in a more efficient and maintainable way. This chapter delves into the foundational concepts of microservices, including how they work, their communication patterns, and how they contribute to creating scalable, resilient applications. We will also explore a real-world example using Netflix, a pioneer in implementing microservices, and guide you through setting up a basic microservice in Node.js and Express to help you start building your own systems.

Key Concepts: Microservices, APIs, Service Communication, and Loose Coupling

Before diving into practical examples, it's important to define key concepts and understand how microservices work in the context of modern software development.

What are Microservices?

At its core, **microservices architecture** is an architectural style where an application is broken down into smaller, independent services. Each of these services is responsible for a specific functionality of the application and can run independently of others. Microservices communicate with each other over the network (usually through HTTP/REST, messaging, or other protocols), and each service can be developed, deployed, and maintained independently.

These services are self-contained, meaning they have their own data store and logic, which allows them to be isolated from the rest of the system. The goal is to have a modular approach where each service is focused on a single business function, such as user authentication, product management, order processing, or payments.

One of the key characteristics of microservices is **loose coupling**. Loose coupling refers to the degree to which services are independent of each other. In a loosely coupled architecture, changes to one service should not directly impact other services. This makes microservices highly scalable, resilient, and easier to maintain, as services can be updated or replaced without disturbing the entire system.

What are APIs?

An **API (Application Programming Interface)** is a set of rules and protocols that allows different software applications to communicate with each other. In a microservices architecture, APIs are used as the primary means of communication between services. Each service exposes a well-defined API, which other services can consume to interact with it.

APIs can be **RESTful** (Representational State Transfer), **SOAP** (Simple Object Access Protocol), or other communication mechanisms, but the most common approach in microservices is REST APIs, especially for web-based services. RESTful APIs use HTTP as the transport protocol and are typically stateless, meaning each request from a client contains all the information necessary to complete the request.

When building microservices, APIs serve as the contract between the services. Each service is responsible for exposing a clean, well-documented API, and other services that need to interact with it do so via these APIs. This decouples the internal workings of the service from the outside world, promoting loose coupling and flexibility.

Service Communication in Microservices

Since microservices are decentralized and self-contained, they rely on communication mechanisms to interact with each other. There are two main types of service communication:

1. **Synchronous Communication:** Synchronous communication occurs when a service directly communicates with another service and waits for a response. This is typically done using HTTP-based protocols such as REST APIs, where a request is sent, and the system waits for a response. If a service doesn't respond quickly enough, it can lead to delays or timeouts. While this method is straightforward and commonly used in microservices, it can introduce challenges related to service dependency and response time.

Example: A **User Service** needs to check if a user has placed an order, so it sends a synchronous REST API request to the **Order Service**. If the Order Service is slow to respond, the User Service might have to wait, causing a delay for the end-user.

2. **Asynchronous Communication:** Asynchronous communication involves sending a request without waiting for an immediate response. Instead, the sender might store a message in a message queue or event stream and continue with other tasks, expecting the receiver to process the message at a later time. This approach decouples the services further and improves resilience, as services don't need to be available at the same time.

Example: The **Payment Service** might send an event to a message queue, notifying other services that a payment has been made. The **Order Service** can process this event asynchronously, without needing to wait for the payment service's response.

Loose Coupling in Microservices

Loose coupling is one of the most important benefits of microservices. In a monolithic system, various modules or components are tightly interdependent. A change in one part of the application often requires changes in many other parts, making it harder to scale, deploy, and maintain.

In a microservices architecture, services are **loosely coupled**, meaning they can evolve independently. Services communicate with each other via well-defined APIs, and a change in one service should not directly affect others. For example, if the **Payment Service** changes how it handles transactions, the **User Service** should not need to change, as long as the Payment Service maintains the same API interface.

The loose coupling enables microservices to be independently scalable, tested, deployed, and updated, making them much more flexible than monolithic systems.

Real-World Example

One of the most well-known examples of microservices in action is Netflix. Netflix uses microservices to handle billions of users, process millions of hours of video streaming, and manage a vast ecosystem of features ranging from user authentication to recommendations, payment processing, and content delivery.

How Netflix Scaled with Microservices

In the early days, Netflix used a monolithic application, which worked well when the user base was small. However, as Netflix grew and its service expanded internationally, it became clear that the monolithic architecture could no longer support the scale and flexibility needed to deliver the content and experiences users expect.

To solve this problem, Netflix moved to a microservices architecture, breaking down their application into hundreds of smaller services that handle different aspects of the platform. For example:

- **User Service:** Handles user login, registration, and profile management.

- **Recommendation Service:** Provides personalized recommendations based on viewing history.

- **Video Streaming Service:** Manages video playback, buffering, and quality.

- **Payment Service:** Manages subscriptions, billing, and payments.

Each of these services operates independently, can be deployed and scaled separately, and can evolve without affecting the others. For instance, the **Video Streaming Service** can be scaled independently to handle peak demand during popular shows or events, while the **Payment Service** can be updated without worrying about how it affects the user interface or streaming quality.

Additionally, Netflix uses asynchronous communication to handle large volumes of data. For instance, Netflix might send event-driven messages when a user adds a movie to their watchlist, and other services, such as recommendations, will process these events asynchronously. This improves performance, reduces latency, and ensures the platform remains responsive even during high traffic periods.

Tutorial: A Simple REST API with Basic Microservice Interaction

Now that we've explored the key concepts and real-world examples of microservices, let's dive into setting up a basic microservice using **Node.js** and **Express**. This microservice will expose a simple API that handles user information and interacts with another service to retrieve user data.

Step 1: Setting Up the Project

Start by creating a new directory for your project and navigate into it:

bash

```
mkdir user-service
cd user-service
```

Next, initialize a new Node.js project:

bash

```bash
npm init -y
```

Install the necessary dependencies, including **Express** for creating the REST API:

bash

```bash
npm install express
```

Step 2: Building the User Service

Create a file called server.js in your project folder. This will be the entry point for your service.

javascript

```javascript
const express = require('express');
const app = express();
const PORT = 3000;

app.use(express.json());

let users = [
    { id: 1, name: 'John Doe', email: 'john@example.com' },
    { id: 2, name: 'Jane Smith', email: 'jane@example.com' }
];
```

```
// Get all users
app.get('/users', (req, res) => {
  res.status(200).json(users);
});

// Get user by ID
app.get('/users/:id', (req, res) => {
  const user = users.find(u => u.id ===
parseInt(req.params.id));
  if (!user) return res.status(404).send('User not found');
  res.status(200).json(user);
});

// Start the server
app.listen(PORT, () => {
  console.log(`User service running on
http://localhost:${PORT}`);
});
```

This code defines two routes: one for getting all users and another for fetching a specific user by ID. The data is stored in an array for simplicity, but in a real-world scenario, this would be connected to a database.

Step 3: Running the Service

Start the server by running:

bash

```
node server.js
```

The service will be accessible on http://localhost:3000. You can test the API using tools like Postman or curl:

- **Get all users**: GET http://localhost:3000/users

- **Get user by ID**: GET http://localhost:3000/users/1

Step 4: Creating a Simple Client Service to Interact with the User Service

Now, let's create another service to interact with the User Service. Create a new folder called client-service and initialize a new Node.js project:

bash

```
mkdir client-service
cd client-service
npm init -y
npm install axios
```

Create a file called client.js:

javascript

```javascript
const axios = require('axios');

const getUser = async (id) => {
  try {
    const response = await
axios.get(`http://localhost:3000/users/${id}`);
    console.log('User data:', response.data);
  } catch (error) {
    console.error('Error fetching user data:', error.message);
  }
};
```

getUser(1);

This client service uses **Axios** to make a GET request to the **User Service** API. When you run the client service, it will fetch the user with ID 1 and display the user data in the console.

Project: Setting Up a Simple Service Using Node.js and Express

By following the tutorial above, you've successfully created two simple services that interact with each other. You've set up:

1. A **User Service** that exposes a REST API to fetch user information.

2. A **Client Service** that consumes the API to retrieve user data.

This setup is a basic illustration of microservices, where each service has its own domain and responsibility. Microservices communicate through APIs, allowing for scalable, flexible, and resilient systems.

Conclusion

In this chapter, we've laid the foundation for understanding microservices architecture, exploring key concepts such as microservices, APIs, service communication, and loose coupling. We also examined a real-world example using Netflix's adoption of microservices to handle millions of users and traffic spikes. Finally, through a hands-on tutorial and project, we set up a basic Node.js and Express service and demonstrated basic microservice interaction.

As you continue to build on this knowledge, you'll be able to develop and deploy more sophisticated microservices systems that scale, integrate seamlessly with other services, and respond dynamically to user needs. Microservices are the future of modern software architecture, and this chapter has set you on the right path to mastering them.

CHAPTER 2: DESIGNING SCALABLE MICROSERVICES

Designing scalable microservices is at the core of building high-performance, resilient, and responsive applications. As applications grow, handling more users, data, and traffic requires a robust architecture capable of scaling seamlessly. In this chapter, we'll dive deep into key principles that govern the design of scalable microservices, such as scalability, fault tolerance, and independent deployability. By understanding these principles, you'll be able to create microservices that can handle large-scale, real-world applications effectively.

We will explore real-world examples, such as how Uber designs its microservices to handle massive amounts of traffic. Additionally, we'll break down the design of a **user authentication microservice**, focusing on its scalability and the ability to deploy independently. Finally, we'll offer actionable insights on how to design microservices that are modular, scalable, and responsive to changing demand.

Key Principles of Scalable Microservices

Building scalable microservices requires a strategic approach to designing each service to handle growth, traffic surges, and failure scenarios. This section covers the foundational principles for designing microservices that scale effectively.

1. Scalability

Scalability is the ability of a system to handle a growing amount of work or its potential to accommodate growth. In the context of microservices, scalability refers to the system's capacity to grow in size and performance without negatively impacting the user experience or system stability.

There are two types of scalability to consider:

- **Vertical Scaling (Scale-Up):** This involves adding more resources (CPU, RAM) to an existing server or container to handle increased load. While simple, vertical scaling has limitations, and there's a ceiling on how much a single server can be upgraded.

- **Horizontal Scaling (Scale-Out):** This is the more common approach for microservices. Horizontal scaling involves adding more instances of the service across multiple machines or containers to distribute the load. It allows services to scale efficiently without running into hardware limitations.

In a microservices architecture, **each service should be designed to scale horizontally**. This means that if traffic increases for one specific service, more instances of that service can be spun up to handle the load. For instance, if your user authentication service begins to see more traffic during peak hours, you can horizontally scale that service by adding additional instances.

To achieve this, microservices should be stateless, meaning each instance can function independently of the others. This allows services to be added or removed from the load balancer pool without affecting performance.

2. Fault Tolerance

In a distributed system, failure is inevitable. Whether it's a network issue, a hardware failure, or a service crashing, microservices must be designed with **fault tolerance** in mind. Fault tolerance ensures that your system continues to operate despite failures, with minimal impact on users.

There are several techniques used to achieve fault tolerance:

- **Redundancy:** By running multiple instances of a service, you ensure that if one instance fails, others can take over. Load balancers are used to distribute traffic across these instances, ensuring continuous availability.

- **Retries and Circuit Breakers:** A common pattern in microservices is using **circuit breakers** and **retry logic** to handle service failures gracefully. If one service fails to respond, the circuit breaker will temporarily stop sending requests to that service, allowing it time to recover. Retries can be used to attempt a failed operation again after a delay, increasing the chance of success.

- **Graceful Degradation:** When part of a system fails, it should degrade gracefully rather than crashing completely. For example, if your recommendation service goes down, the e-commerce platform might show a default set of recommendations rather than showing no recommendations at all.

- **Health Checks:** Regular health checks for microservices can help detect issues early. If a service fails its health check, it can be automatically restarted or replaced with a healthy instance.

A good example of fault tolerance can be seen in **Netflix**, which uses multiple redundant instances of its microservices and employs strategies like retries and circuit breakers to ensure that its platform remains operational even in the face of partial failures.

3. Independent Deployability

One of the primary benefits of microservices is the ability to **deploy services independently**. Each service in a microservices architecture is a self-contained unit, with its own database, logic, and API. This independence means that teams can develop, test, and deploy services without affecting the rest of the system.

The ability to deploy services independently provides several key benefits:

- **Faster Time to Market:** Independent deployability allows teams to release updates or new features for a specific service without waiting for the entire application to be ready. This results in faster iteration and reduced downtime.

- **Minimized Risk:** When a service is deployed independently, the impact of a failure is limited to that service, rather than the entire application. This reduces the risk of introducing bugs or outages in other parts of the system.

- **Continuous Delivery and CI/CD:** With microservices, you can set up continuous delivery pipelines to deploy changes as soon as they are ready. Each service has its own pipeline, which can be automated using CI/CD tools like Jenkins, GitLab CI, or CircleCI.

- **No Long Dependencies:** In traditional monolithic architectures, you often need to wait for multiple teams to coordinate changes before deploying a new feature. With microservices, you only need to update the service in question, and other services can continue to operate independently.

The independence of deployment also makes it easier to maintain microservices in production. Services can be updated, scaled, or replaced without worrying about affecting the rest of the system.

Real-World Example

Uber is a prime example of a company that has scaled successfully using microservices. Initially, Uber's application was monolithic, which made it difficult to scale. As the company grew and began handling millions of users, Uber realized that it needed to break its system into smaller, more manageable services to handle the growing complexity and traffic.

Challenges Faced by Uber

- **High Traffic Load:** During peak times, Uber handles millions of user requests, from ride requests to driver availability and payment processing.

- **Global Scaling:** Uber operates in multiple cities around the world, each with different traffic patterns, languages, and payment systems.

- **Real-Time Data:** Uber must process real-time data such as location, availability, and traffic patterns to provide timely and accurate ride information.

How Uber Uses Microservices

Uber transitioned to a microservices architecture to handle these challenges. It decomposed its monolithic application into a series of microservices, each responsible for specific aspects of the system:

- **Ride Request Service:** This service manages ride requests, matching drivers to passengers based on proximity.

- **Payment Service:** Handles all payment-related tasks, including pricing, payment processing, and refunds.

- **Driver Service:** Manages driver registration, availability, and route optimizations.

- **Location Service:** Uses real-time location data to match riders and drivers, calculate fares, and provide estimated times of arrival.

Uber's microservices are designed to be highly scalable, and the company uses containerization (via **Docker**) and orchestration (via **Kubernetes**) to scale these services dynamically based on traffic. For instance, if a particular city experiences a surge in ride requests, the Ride Request Service can be scaled independently to handle the increased load without affecting other services like Payment or Driver Services.

Additionally, Uber employs **event-driven communication** between services. For example, when a ride request is placed, an event is emitted that other services can listen to. The **Payment Service** listens for the event and triggers payment processing when a ride is completed. This asynchronous communication ensures that services remain loosely coupled and can scale independently.

The Results

By adopting a microservices architecture, Uber was able to:

- **Scale efficiently** to handle millions of requests per minute.

- **Minimize downtime** during peak traffic periods.

- **Improve fault tolerance**, as failures in one service do not bring down the entire platform.

- **Deploy services independently**, enabling faster iteration and new feature releases.

Tutorial: Breaking Down the Design of a User Authentication Microservice

Let's now walk through the design of a user authentication microservice. The goal of this microservice is to handle user sign-up, login, and session management. We will design it with scalability, fault tolerance, and independent deployability in mind.

Step 1: Service Requirements

The user authentication service will need to:

- **Allow users to register** with an email and password.

- **Authenticate users** by verifying credentials and issuing a JWT (JSON Web Token) for secure access.

- **Manage sessions**, ensuring that users are logged in and able to make authorized requests.

To scale this service, we must ensure that it is **stateless**. Each request should contain the necessary information (such as a token) to authenticate the user, so there is no dependency on a central session store.

Step 2: Service Architecture

- **API Endpoints:**

    o POST /auth/register: For user registration.

    o POST /auth/login: For user login and token generation.

    o GET /auth/me: For retrieving user profile information using the JWT.

- **Database:** We'll use a simple relational database like **PostgreSQL** to store user data, such as email and hashed password. However, as the service scales, we could switch to NoSQL if needed for flexibility.

- **Token-Based Authentication:** We'll use JWT for stateless authentication. This allows each request to carry the user's identity in the form of a token, which can be verified by the service.

- **Fault Tolerance:** To ensure the service is resilient, we will implement retry logic for database calls, especially when network latency occurs. We'll also use a circuit breaker pattern to prevent cascading failures.

Step 3: Building the Service with Node.js and Express

Let's start by setting up a basic Node.js application using Express.

bash

```
mkdir auth-service
cd auth-service
npm init -y
npm install express jsonwebtoken bcryptjs pg
```

Now, create a file server.js to define the API.

javascript

```
const express = require('express');
const bcrypt = require('bcryptjs');
const jwt = require('jsonwebtoken');
const { Pool } = require('pg');

const app = express();
```

```javascript
const pool = new Pool({
  user: 'your_user',
  host: 'localhost',
  database: 'auth_db',
  password: 'your_password',
  port: 5432,
});

app.use(express.json());

// User Registration
app.post('/auth/register', async (req, res) => {
  const { email, password } = req.body;
  const hashedPassword = await bcrypt.hash(password, 10);

  const result = await pool.query('INSERT INTO users (email,
password) VALUES ($1, $2) RETURNING *', [email,
hashedPassword]);
  res.status(201).json({ user: result.rows[0] });
});

// User Login
```

```javascript
app.post('/auth/login', async (req, res) => {
  const { email, password } = req.body;

  const result = await pool.query('SELECT * FROM users
WHERE email = $1', [email]);
  if (!result.rows.length) {
    return res.status(400).send('Invalid credentials');
  }

  const user = result.rows[0];
  const match = await bcrypt.compare(password,
user.password);
  if (!match) {
    return res.status(400).send('Invalid credentials');
  }

  const token = jwt.sign({ userId: user.id }, 'your_jwt_secret',
{ expiresIn: '1h' });
  res.json({ token });
});

// Get User Profile
```

```
app.get('/auth/me', async (req, res) => {
  const token = req.headers.authorization?.split(' ')[1];
  if (!token) return res.status(401).send('Unauthorized');

  try {
    const decoded = jwt.verify(token, 'your_jwt_secret');
    const result = await pool.query('SELECT * FROM users
WHERE id = $1', [decoded.userId]);
    res.json({ user: result.rows[0] });
  } catch (error) {
    res.status(401).send('Unauthorized');
  }
});

app.listen(3000, () => {
  console.log('Auth service running on http://localhost:3000');
});
```

This is a basic authentication service that registers users, authenticates them with JWT, and retrieves user profiles.

Actionable Insight: Designing Microservices for Scalability

When designing microservices, always think about **independence, statelessness**, and **modularity**. Each service should have a clear responsibility and be able to scale independently to meet the demand. Additionally, **use event-driven architectures** and **asynchronous communication** to decouple services and make them more resilient.

By designing services that are stateless, horizontally scalable, and independently deployable, you can ensure that your application can handle high traffic and adapt to changes as the system evolves.

This chapter provided a foundation for designing scalable microservices by covering core principles, real-world examples like Uber, and a hands-on tutorial for creating a user authentication microservice. In the next chapter, we will delve deeper into service communication patterns and explore how to build robust APIs for microservices.

CHAPTER 3: SERVICE COMMUNICATION IN MICROSERVICES

One of the most critical aspects of building microservices is how services communicate with one another. In a microservices architecture, services are designed to be independent, but they still need to collaborate and share data. The communication between these distributed services is essential for ensuring that data flows seamlessly and the system remains consistent and responsive.

In this chapter, we'll dive deep into the different types of communication in microservices, focusing on **synchronous** vs. **asynchronous communication**, and explore the concept of **event-driven architecture**. We will also look at a real-world example of how **Slack** utilizes message queues to handle real-time communication, and then walk through setting up a message queue using **RabbitMQ**. Lastly, we'll create a project that implements two services, one that sends messages to a queue and another that consumes them.

Types of Communication in Microservices

In microservices, communication between services is typically categorized into two types:

1. **Synchronous Communication**

2. **Asynchronous Communication**

Understanding when and how to use each type of communication is critical for building efficient, scalable, and fault-tolerant microservices. Each has its advantages and trade-offs, and selecting the right type depends on the specific needs of the application.

Synchronous Communication

Synchronous communication occurs when one service sends a request to another service and waits for a response before proceeding. This type of communication is usually implemented using **RESTful APIs, gRPC**, or **SOAP** (although REST is by far the most common in modern microservices). Synchronous communication is often used in situations where the requesting service needs immediate feedback from the responding service to continue processing.

Key Characteristics of Synchronous Communication:

- **Blocking:** The calling service sends a request and waits for a response. During this time, the calling service is blocked until it receives a reply.

- **Direct Communication:** Services communicate directly, often over HTTP or another transport protocol like gRPC.

- **Tight Coupling:** Because one service depends on the response from another, there's a greater degree of coupling between the services. If one service is unavailable or slow, it impacts the calling service.

Advantages of Synchronous Communication:

- **Immediate Feedback:** The calling service receives an immediate response, making this type of communication useful when the requesting service needs to proceed based on the response.

- **Simple and Easy to Implement:** Synchronous APIs (especially RESTful ones) are straightforward to implement and test, making them suitable for simple tasks like retrieving data or updating a resource.

Disadvantages of Synchronous Communication:

- **Performance Bottleneck:** If a service is slow to respond or experiences downtime, it can cause significant delays or even failures in the entire system.

- **Scalability Issues:** Because services are tightly coupled, scaling synchronous communication can be difficult. If one service is overwhelmed with requests, the entire system may experience degradation in performance.

- **Reliability Concerns:** If a service fails to respond or crashes, the requesting service will typically fail as well, which could lead to a cascading failure in the system.

Use Cases for Synchronous Communication:

Synchronous communication is best suited for scenarios where the requestor needs real-time data or immediate results to proceed, such as:

- **Fetching data from a database** (e.g., user profiles or product details).

- **User authentication** (where a response is required to validate the login).

- **Order processing systems** where real-time decision-making is critical.

Asynchronous Communication

Asynchronous communication occurs when one service sends a request to another service but does not wait for a response. Instead, the service continues its process and may later handle the response when it arrives. This approach is commonly implemented using message queues or event-driven systems, where services communicate by sending messages to a queue or a stream and then processing them in the background.

Key Characteristics of Asynchronous Communication:

- **Non-Blocking:** The calling service does not wait for a response. It sends a message and moves on, enabling it to continue processing other tasks.

- **Event-Driven:** Asynchronous communication often involves events, where a service publishes an event to signal that something has happened (e.g., "order placed" or "user registered").

- **Loose Coupling:** Services do not directly communicate with each other. Instead, they communicate via a queue or event stream, reducing the dependencies between them.

Advantages of Asynchronous Communication:

- **Decoupling of Services:** Because services do not directly communicate, they are less dependent on each other's availability and performance. This leads to greater resilience in the system.

- **Improved Performance and Scalability:** Since services do not need to wait for responses, they can handle a higher volume of requests and be more responsive under heavy load.

- **Reliability and Fault Tolerance:** If a service fails, the message or event can be retried or processed later, ensuring that the system continues to function even during temporary outages.

Disadvantages of Asynchronous Communication:

- **Complexity:** Asynchronous communication can be more difficult to manage and debug, as the system requires more infrastructure to handle queues, events, and message processing.

- **Latency:** While asynchronous communication allows for faster throughput, there may be a delay between the time a message is sent and when the service processes it.

Use Cases for Asynchronous Communication:

Asynchronous communication is well-suited for scenarios where the service does not need an immediate response to proceed. Some common use cases include:

- **Order processing and payment systems** where the request does not need to be immediately validated but can be processed in the background.

- **Sending emails or notifications** after a user action has been completed (e.g., a confirmation email after an order).

- **Event-driven architectures** where actions in the system (e.g., a user signing up or a payment being made) trigger further processes.

Event-Driven Architecture

Event-driven architecture (EDA) is a design pattern in which services communicate by emitting and consuming events. An **event** is simply a signal that something of interest has occurred within the system. An event can represent anything from a user action (like placing an order) to a system update (such as a product being restocked).

Key Components of Event-Driven Architecture:

1. **Event Producer:** The service that generates and emits events. For example, when a user places an order, the **Order Service** might emit an event called order_placed.

2. **Event Channel:** This is the communication medium that allows services to transmit events. Examples include message queues, event streams, or Kafka topics. The event channel ensures that events can be reliably transmitted and consumed by interested services.

3. **Event Consumer:** The service that listens for events and reacts to them. For instance, after the **Order Service** emits the order_placed event, the **Inventory Service** may consume that event to decrement the stock levels.

Advantages of Event-Driven Architecture:

- **Scalability:** By decoupling services, EDA allows each service to scale independently. Events can be processed in parallel, and services can handle varying loads efficiently.

- **Flexibility:** New services can be added to listen for and respond to events without impacting existing services, making the system more adaptable.

- **Fault Tolerance:** Events can be stored temporarily and retried if a consumer service is down or facing issues, ensuring data integrity.

Challenges of Event-Driven Architecture:

- **Eventual Consistency:** Since events are processed asynchronously, achieving consistency across services can be challenging. Systems need to be designed to handle situations where different services might be temporarily out of sync.

- **Complexity in Debugging:** Since events don't return immediate results, tracking the flow of events and ensuring they are processed correctly can be difficult.

Real-World Example

Slack, the popular team collaboration tool, handles millions of messages and notifications in real-time across various channels and direct messages. To ensure that the platform remains responsive and scalable, Slack uses **message queues** as part of its architecture.

Slack's Use of Message Queues:

- **Real-Time Notifications:** When a message is sent in Slack, it must be delivered to all users who are subscribed to the relevant channel. To handle this efficiently, Slack uses message queues to manage these real-time notifications and ensure they are delivered even under heavy load.

- **Event-Driven Architecture:** Slack's backend is event-driven, meaning when a user sends a message, an event is emitted. This event triggers a series of downstream processes, including message delivery, logging, and notifications.

- **Decoupling Services:** By using message queues, Slack decouples its services, allowing individual services (like user authentication, message delivery, and notifications) to operate independently while still sharing data asynchronously.

The use of message queues in Slack's architecture helps handle millions of messages per second, making the platform highly scalable and resilient even during traffic spikes.

Tutorial: Setting Up a Message Queue Using RabbitMQ

Let's dive into setting up a message queue using **RabbitMQ**, one of the most widely-used open-source message brokers. RabbitMQ implements the Advanced Message Queuing Protocol (AMQP), which enables reliable communication between services.

Step 1: Installing RabbitMQ

To get started, install RabbitMQ. If you're using Docker, it's as simple as running:

bash

```
docker run -d -p 5672:5672 -p 15672:15672 --name rabbitmq
rabbitmq:management
```

This command will run RabbitMQ and expose the management interface on port 15672, and the AMQP protocol on port 5672.

Alternatively, if you're installing RabbitMQ on your local machine, follow the installation guide.

Step 2: Sending Messages to a Queue

Now let's implement a simple service that sends messages to a RabbitMQ queue. Create a file send.js and install the amqplib package:

bash

```
npm install amqplib
```

javascript

```javascript
const amqp = require('amqplib/callback_api');

amqp.connect('amqp://localhost', (error0, connection) => {
  if (error0) {
    throw error0;
  }
  connection.createChannel((error1, channel) => {
    if (error1) {
      throw error1;
    }
    const queue = 'hello';
    const msg = 'Hello World!';

    channel.assertQueue(queue, {
      durable: false
    });

    channel.sendToQueue(queue, Buffer.from(msg));
    console.log(" [x] Sent %s", msg);
  });
});
```

This script connects to RabbitMQ, creates a channel, and sends a "Hello World!" message to a queue named hello.

Step 3: Consuming Messages from the Queue

Next, let's create a simple service that consumes messages from the queue. Create a file receive.js:

javascript

```javascript
const amqp = require('amqplib/callback_api');

amqp.connect('amqp://localhost', (error0, connection) => {
  if (error0) {
    throw error0;
  }
  connection.createChannel((error1, channel) => {
    if (error1) {
      throw error1;
    }
    const queue = 'hello';

    channel.assertQueue(queue, {
```

```
    durable: false
  });

  console.log(" [*] Waiting for messages in %s. To exit press
CTRL+C", queue);

  channel.consume(queue, (msg) => {
    console.log(" [x] Received %s", msg.content.toString());
  }, {
    noAck: true
  });
  });
});
```

This script connects to RabbitMQ, listens for messages on the hello queue, and logs any received messages to the console.

Step 4: Running the Services

1. First, run the receive.js script in one terminal:

```bash
node receive.js
```

2. Then, in another terminal, run the send.js script to send a message:

bash

node send.js

You should see the message "Hello World!" appear in the consumer service's console.

Project: Implementing a Simple Service with Message Queues

Now that you've set up RabbitMQ and created a basic message-sending and message-consuming system, you can experiment by extending this project with more advanced functionality. For instance, you could add:

- Multiple services consuming from different queues.

- Message retries or dead-letter queues for failed messages.

- Scaling the producer or consumer services to handle higher loads.

Conclusion

In this chapter, we've explored the various types of communication in microservices, including **synchronous** and **asynchronous** communication, and introduced **event-driven architecture** as a powerful design pattern for building scalable and resilient systems. We examined how **Slack** uses message queues to handle real-time communication, and we provided a hands-on tutorial on setting up RabbitMQ to facilitate communication between services.

The key takeaway is that **asynchronous communication** and **event-driven architecture** allow microservices to scale efficiently, remain resilient under heavy loads, and decouple services for greater flexibility. By understanding these patterns and tools, you'll be better equipped to build robust, scalable microservices systems.

CHAPTER 4:
CHOOSING THE
RIGHT DATABASE
FOR MICROSERVICES

In the world of microservices, choosing the right database architecture is just as critical as selecting the right technologies for building the services themselves. Unlike monolithic applications, where a single relational database might suffice for the entire application, microservices introduce new challenges. Each service is designed to be independent, which means that each service may have different data storage needs, which is where **polyglot persistence** comes into play. The idea is that different types of data and use cases should be handled by the most appropriate database technology.

This chapter will explore the fundamental concepts of polyglot persistence, real-world examples, such as **eBay's use of multiple databases**, and practical guidance on how to integrate and manage multiple databases in your microservices architecture. We'll also provide a hands-on tutorial using **MongoDB** for a user service and **PostgreSQL** for a product inventory service, along with a project to integrate databases into your microservices for persistence.

Key Concepts: Polyglot Persistence

In the context of microservices, **polyglot persistence** refers to the practice of using different types of databases to store different kinds of data within the same system. This stands in stark contrast to the traditional monolithic approach where a single database is used for the entire application. Microservices, with their diverse and specialized nature, benefit from the flexibility of choosing the right database for the right task. Let's break down why this approach is necessary and how it is implemented.

Why Polyglot Persistence Matters in Microservices

1. **Different Data Models:** Each service in a microservices architecture typically has a specific, narrow focus. Some services may need to store data that is highly relational, while others may need to store large amounts of unstructured or semi-structured data. Traditional databases like **SQL databases** (e.g., **PostgreSQL, MySQL**) are great for

structured, relational data. However, other types of data might be better suited for **NoSQL databases** (e.g., **MongoDB**, **Cassandra**) or **key-value stores** (e.g., **Redis**).

- o **Relational Data:** Services that need to maintain complex relationships between entities (e.g., user profiles, product details) often benefit from SQL databases with ACID compliance.

- o **Unstructured Data:** Services that manage data like logs, sensor data, or messages (e.g., in a chat application) might be better served with NoSQL databases that are designed for large volumes of unstructured or semi-structured data.

- o **Key-Value Stores:** Services that require fast read/write operations for simple data like caching or session management benefit from key-value stores like Redis or Memcached.

2. **Scalability:** Different databases offer varying levels of scalability. NoSQL databases, for instance, are designed to handle massive amounts of data and can be horizontally scaled across multiple nodes. In contrast, SQL databases are often vertically scaled, meaning you add more resources (CPU, memory) to

a single machine, which can become a bottleneck as the system grows.

3. **Decentralized Control:** Since each microservice is independent, they can choose the database that best meets their needs without having to rely on a centralized data model. This autonomy reduces bottlenecks and improves agility, as services can evolve their data models independently.

4. **Optimizing Performance:** By choosing the right database for each service, you can optimize the performance of the application overall. For instance, a product catalog service might require a **graph database** for complex relationships, whereas an order management service might only need a **relational database** to track transactions.

5. **Data Isolation and Independence:** Microservices are designed to be isolated and independently deployable. By using separate databases for each service, you ensure that changes to one service's data model don't affect the others, allowing you to update or scale services independently.

Types of Databases in Polyglot Persistence

To better understand polyglot persistence, let's look at some common types of databases used in microservices architectures:

1. **Relational Databases (SQL):**

   o **Examples:** PostgreSQL, MySQL, SQL Server

   o **Use Case:** Services that need structured data, strong consistency, and complex relationships between entities.

   o **Strengths:** ACID transactions, complex joins, and reporting capabilities.

2. **Document Stores (NoSQL):**

   o **Examples:** MongoDB, CouchDB

   o **Use Case:** Services that store semi-structured data or require schema flexibility, like user profiles, logs, or product catalogs.

   o **Strengths:** Scalability, flexibility, and performance for large datasets.

3. **Key-Value Stores:**

   o **Examples:** Redis, Memcached

   o **Use Case:** Services that need fast access to data with minimal complexity, such as caching, session storage, or temporary data storage.

- o **Strengths:** Extremely fast read/write operations, particularly for non-complex data.

4. **Graph Databases:**

   - o **Examples:** Neo4j, ArangoDB

   - o **Use Case:** Services that require traversing complex relationships between entities, like social networks or recommendation engines.

   - o **Strengths:** Efficient for querying and managing highly connected data.

5. **Columnar Databases:**

   - o **Examples:** Cassandra, HBase

   - o **Use Case:** Services that need to handle very large amounts of distributed data, such as telemetry data or large-scale analytics.

   - o **Strengths:** Highly scalable, great for write-heavy and read-heavy workloads.

Real-World Example

eBay is a prime example of a company that has implemented polyglot persistence in its microservices architecture. As one of the world's largest online marketplaces, eBay needs to handle massive volumes of data across its services, and different types of data require different storage mechanisms.

Challenges Faced by eBay

- **Massive User Base:** eBay serves millions of users globally, each with unique product listings, search histories, and purchase behaviors.

- **Diverse Data Needs:** Different types of data (e.g., transactional data, product listings, user preferences) require different storage approaches to ensure both scalability and performance.

- **Fast Response Times:** As an e-commerce platform, eBay needs to provide fast responses, particularly during sales events, and must ensure that services are always available.

How eBay Uses Polyglot Persistence

eBay uses multiple databases to handle different types of data effectively:

- **Relational Databases (SQL):** eBay uses **MySQL** to manage transactional data, such as user orders and payment processing. SQL databases are used for data that requires strong consistency and relational integrity.

- **NoSQL Databases:** For more flexible and scalable storage, eBay uses **Cassandra** to handle product listings, user sessions, and catalog data. Cassandra's horizontal scalability allows eBay to handle massive amounts of data without compromising performance.

- **Search Services:** For search indexing and queries, eBay uses **Elasticsearch** to provide fast and scalable search capabilities across millions of product listings and user interactions.

- **Caching with Key-Value Stores:** eBay uses **Redis** to cache frequently accessed data, such as search results, product recommendations, and user profiles, to ensure low-latency responses.

- **Analytics and Big Data Processing:** eBay uses **Hadoop** and **Spark** to process and analyze large datasets, allowing the company to gain insights into user behavior and market trends.

By leveraging different databases for different services, eBay is able to maintain high performance, scalability, and reliability across its platform, providing an optimal experience for users and sellers alike.

Tutorial: Using MongoDB for a User Service and PostgreSQL for a Product Inventory Service

Let's dive into a hands-on tutorial where we'll build two services using **MongoDB** for a user service and **PostgreSQL** for a product inventory service. This example demonstrates how polyglot persistence can be used to meet the specific needs of different services.

Step 1: Setting Up MongoDB for the User Service

1. **Install MongoDB:**

If you haven't already installed MongoDB, you can do so using Docker or directly on your machine. To run MongoDB with Docker, use:

bash

```
docker run -d -p 27017:27017 --name mongodb mongo:latest
```

2. **Create the User Service:**

Let's set up a basic Express-based user service that stores user data in **MongoDB**. First, initialize a new project:

bash

```bash
mkdir user-service
cd user-service
npm init -y
npm install express mongoose
```

3. Create the user.js Model:

Create a models/user.js file for the user schema.

javascript

```javascript
const mongoose = require('mongoose');

const userSchema = new mongoose.Schema({
  name: { type: String, required: true },
  email: { type: String, required: true, unique: true },
  password: { type: String, required: true },
});

module.exports = mongoose.model('User', userSchema);
```

4. Set Up the User API:

In your server.js file, connect to MongoDB and create basic endpoints for adding and fetching users.

```javascript
const express = require('express');
const mongoose = require('mongoose');
const User = require('./models/user');

const app = express();
app.use(express.json());

mongoose.connect('mongodb://localhost:27017/userdb', {
useNewUrlParser: true, useUnifiedTopology: true });

app.post('/users', async (req, res) => {
  const { name, email, password } = req.body;
  const user = new User({ name, email, password });
  await user.save();
  res.status(201).send(user);
});

app.get('/users', async (req, res) => {
  const users = await User.find();
  res.status(200).send(users);
```

```
});

app.listen(3001, () => {
  console.log('User service running on http://localhost:3001');
});
```

Step 2: Setting Up PostgreSQL for the Product Inventory Service

1. **Install PostgreSQL:**

If you don't have PostgreSQL installed, you can use Docker to run it:

bash

```
docker run -d -p 5432:5432 --name postgres postgres
```

2. **Create the Product Service:**

Set up a basic Express-based product inventory service that stores product data in **PostgreSQL**. First, initialize the project:

bash

```
mkdir product-service
cd product-service
```

```
npm init -y
```

```
npm install express pg
```

3. Create the product.js Model:

Create a models/product.js file for the product schema.

javascript

```javascript
const { Pool } = require('pg');

const pool = new Pool({
  user: 'postgres',
  host: 'localhost',
  database: 'inventorydb',
  password: 'password',
  port: 5432,
});

const createProductTable = async () => {
  await pool.query(`
    CREATE TABLE IF NOT EXISTS products (
      id SERIAL PRIMARY KEY,
      name VARCHAR(100),
      quantity INTEGER
```

```javascript
  );
 `);
};

const addProduct = async (name, quantity) => {
  const res = await pool.query('INSERT INTO products
(name, quantity) VALUES ($1, $2) RETURNING *', [name,
quantity]);
  return res.rows[0];
};

const getProducts = async () => {
  const res = await pool.query('SELECT * FROM products');
  return res.rows;
};

module.exports = { createProductTable, addProduct,
getProducts };
```

4. **Set Up the Product API:**

In your server.js file, set up the product API.

javascript

```javascript
const express = require('express');
const { createProductTable, addProduct, getProducts } =
require('./models/product');

const app = express();
app.use(express.json());

createProductTable();

app.post('/products', async (req, res) => {
  const { name, quantity } = req.body;
  const product = await addProduct(name, quantity);
  res.status(201).send(product);
});

app.get('/products', async (req, res) => {
  const products = await getProducts();
  res.status(200).send(products);
});

app.listen(3002, () => {
```

```
  console.log('Product service running on
http://localhost:3002');
});
```

Step 3: Integrating the Databases

In this example, we have two separate services, one using **MongoDB** for user management and the other using **PostgreSQL** for product inventory. Both services run independently, with their respective databases, and offer CRUD operations through simple REST APIs. This integration showcases how microservices can use different databases, each optimized for its data and performance needs.

Project: Integrating Databases into Your Microservices for Persistence

Building on this tutorial, you can extend the architecture to include more complex database integrations:

- **Handling Complex Data Types:** For example, you could add features like product categories in the product service or include hashed passwords in the user service.

- **Data Consistency Across Services:** While MongoDB and PostgreSQL are both used for persistence, you might need to sync or replicate data between services for consistency.

- **Eventual Consistency and CQRS:** Implement patterns like **Event Sourcing** and **Command Query Responsibility Segregation** (CQRS) to handle complex data consistency issues in your microservices architecture.

In this project, you have learned how to integrate MongoDB and PostgreSQL into your microservices, enabling each service to operate with the most appropriate database technology for its needs. This flexibility is one of the key advantages of microservices, allowing you to optimize your system for scalability, performance, and maintainability.

CHAPTER 5: SECURING MICROSERVICES COMMUNICATION

In a distributed microservices architecture, securing communication between services is paramount. As microservices systems grow in complexity, so do the challenges of ensuring that the data exchanged between services remains confidential, authentic, and intact. Microservices require robust security measures not only to protect the communication channels but also to ensure that each service is accessible only to authorized users or services.

In this chapter, we will explore the key concepts of **security in microservices**, focusing on **service-to-service authentication** and **authorization**. We'll look at how **Google** secures its microservices in its cloud environment and provide a hands-on tutorial on implementing **JWT (JSON Web Tokens)** for authentication between services. Lastly, we'll build a simple, secured API service using JWT for service-to-service communication.

Key Concepts: Security in Microservices

Microservices architecture is inherently complex due to the large number of independently deployed services that need to interact. The security concerns for these systems go beyond traditional security mechanisms used in monolithic applications. In microservices, we need to think about several key security areas:

1. **Service-to-Service Authentication**

2. **Service Authorization**

3. **Data Privacy and Integrity**

4. **Access Control and Identity Management**

Let's break down these concepts in more detail:

1. Service-to-Service Authentication

Service-to-service authentication refers to ensuring that each service in the microservices architecture is who it says it is before allowing communication to take place. This process is crucial for ensuring that only authorized services can access other services, preventing unauthorized services from hijacking communications.

A common method of achieving service-to-service authentication is by using **JWT (JSON Web Tokens)**. JWT allows a service to issue a signed token containing user or service identity claims, which can then be passed between services to prove identity. This form of token-based authentication is stateless, making it ideal for distributed systems like microservices.

2. Service Authorization

Once authentication is in place, the next step is **authorization**. Authorization ensures that a service has the appropriate permissions to access the resources it is requesting. In the context of microservices, services should not have access to all resources but rather only those that are relevant to their functionality.

This is typically managed through the use of **role-based access control (RBAC)** or **attribute-based access control (ABAC)**. With RBAC, a service is granted roles with specific permissions, and with ABAC, permissions are based on attributes such as service identity, user context, and environment.

For example, if a **user service** authenticates using a JWT, the token might contain claims such as the user's roles and permissions. When the service attempts to access a resource, such as a **product service**, the **product service** will check the user's roles and permissions to decide if the request should be authorized.

3. Data Privacy and Integrity

Microservices communicate over potentially untrusted networks, making it critical to ensure that data is not intercepted or tampered with during transmission. This is where **TLS (Transport Layer Security)** comes into play. TLS ensures that communication between services is encrypted, preventing eavesdropping and tampering.

In addition to encrypting data in transit, it's equally important to ensure that data remains **integral** and has not been altered during transmission. This can be achieved by using cryptographic techniques such as message authentication codes (MACs) or digital signatures.

4. Access Control and Identity Management

Managing identities and access control in a microservices architecture requires a centralized system for identity management. This is commonly achieved through the use of an **Identity Provider (IdP)** and tools like **OAuth2** and **OpenID Connect (OIDC)**.

OAuth2 allows secure, token-based access to APIs and services. OIDC, built on top of OAuth2, provides an authentication layer to ensure that users or services are who they say they are. An IdP such as **Auth0** or **Okta** can handle the heavy lifting of authentication, reducing the complexity for each individual microservice.

Real-World Example

Google provides a fantastic real-world example of securing microservices through its **Google Cloud Platform (GCP)**. Google uses a combination of technologies, including identity management, service-to-service authentication, and API security, to secure communication between its microservices.

Google Cloud Security Stack

1. **Identity and Access Management (IAM):** Google uses IAM to control which services and users can access resources in the Google Cloud environment. Services authenticate via service accounts, which are identities tied to specific services in the cloud.

2. **Istio for Service Mesh:** Google uses **Istio**, an open-source service mesh, to manage and secure service-to-service communication. Istio provides out-of-the-box capabilities for **mutual TLS** authentication between services, encryption of traffic, and role-based access control.

3. **JWT for Authentication:** For securing communication between microservices, Google uses JWT tokens, issued by a central identity provider like **Google Identity Platform**. These tokens allow services to authenticate each other and grant access based on roles and permissions.

4. **API Gateway for Authorization:** Google uses API gateways (such as **Apigee** or **Kong**) to manage the flow of traffic between external clients and microservices. The API Gateway handles **OAuth2 authentication** and **API rate limiting** to protect services from abuse.

5. **TLS for Encryption:** All communication between services in Google Cloud is encrypted using **mTLS** (mutual TLS), ensuring that only authorized services can communicate securely.

By employing these techniques, Google ensures that its microservices can communicate securely while maintaining strong access controls and data integrity.

Tutorial: Implementing JWT Authentication Between Two Services

In this tutorial, we'll implement a simple **JWT-based authentication** system between two services. One service will authenticate users and issue JWT tokens, and the other will validate these tokens to authenticate users for further communication.

Step 1: Set Up the Project

Let's set up two simple services using **Node.js** and **Express**:

1. **User Service (Authentication Service)**: This service will handle user login, generate a JWT token, and send it back to the client.

2. **Product Service (Secured API Service)**: This service will require a valid JWT token for accessing its endpoints.

First, create two directories:

bash

```
mkdir user-service product-service
```

Step 2: User Service

1. Initialize the User Service:

In the user-service directory, run the following command to initialize a Node.js project:

bash

```
cd user-service
npm init -y
npm install express jsonwebtoken bcryptjs
```

2. Create the User Service API:

Create a server.js file in the user-service directory:

javascript

```
const express = require('express');
const jwt = require('jsonwebtoken');
const bcrypt = require('bcryptjs');

const app = express();
const port = 3001;

app.use(express.json());

const users = [
```

```
  { id: 1, username: 'john_doe', password:
'$2a$10$TjWxENFj31nFS1QfM5xv0uQbdggFq0lTPg.V6Mj
Yhr5IlyNXT43mu' }, // password: 'password123'
];

// User login to generate JWT
app.post('/login', async (req, res) => {
  const { username, password } = req.body;

  const user = users.find(u => u.username === username);
  if (!user) return res.status(400).send('User not found');

  const isMatch = await bcrypt.compare(password,
user.password);
  if (!isMatch) return res.status(400).send('Invalid
credentials');

  const token = jwt.sign({ userId: user.id, username:
user.username }, 'secretKey', { expiresIn: '1h' });
  res.json({ token });
});
```

```
app.listen(port, () => {
  console.log(`User Service running at
http://localhost:${port}`);
});
```

In this code:

- A sample user is created with a hashed password (password123).

- The /login route authenticates the user and returns a **JWT token**.

Step 3: Product Service (Secured API Service)

1. **Initialize the Product Service:**

Navigate to the product-service directory and run:

bash

```
cd product-service
npm init -y
npm install express jsonwebtoken
```

2. **Create the Product Service API:**

Create a server.js file in the product-service directory:

```javascript
const express = require('express');
const jwt = require('jsonwebtoken');

const app = express();
const port = 3002;

app.use(express.json());

// Middleware to verify JWT token
const verifyToken = (req, res, next) => {
  const token = req.header('Authorization');
  if (!token) return res.status(403).send('Access denied');

  jwt.verify(token, 'secretKey', (err, decoded) => {
    if (err) return res.status(400).send('Invalid token');
    req.user = decoded;
    next();
  });
};
```

```
// Secured product endpoint
app.get('/products', verifyToken, (req, res) => {
  res.json({ message: 'Product data accessed successfully',
user: req.user });
});


app.listen(port, () => {
  console.log(`Product Service running at
http://localhost:${port}`);
});
```

In this code:

- The verifyToken middleware checks if the incoming request contains a valid JWT token.

- If the token is valid, it proceeds to the secured /products endpoint; otherwise, it denies access.

Step 4: Running the Services

Now, you can start both services:

1. Start the **User Service**:

```bash
bash


node user-service/server.js
```

2. Start the **Product Service**:

bash

```
node product-service/server.js
```

Step 5: Testing the Communication

1. **Login and Get the JWT Token:**

Use a tool like **Postman** or **cURL** to send a POST request to the **User Service**'s /login endpoint:

bash

```
POST http://localhost:3001/login
{
  "username": "john_doe",
  "password": "password123"
}
```

If successful, you'll get a JWT token in the response.

2. **Access the Secured Endpoint:**

Now, use the token to send a GET request to the **Product Service**'s /products endpoint:

bash

GET http://localhost:3002/products

Authorization: Bearer <your-jwt-token>

If the token is valid, the service will respond with the product data. If the token is invalid or missing, the service will return an error.

Project: Create a Simple Secured API Service with JWT

This project demonstrates the core concepts of **service-to-service authentication** in a microservices environment using **JWT**. By creating the **User Service** and **Product Service**, we learned how to:

1. Implement a **login mechanism** to generate a JWT token.

2. Use JWT for **service-to-service authentication**, ensuring that only authorized requests can access secured endpoints.

3. Secure the **Product Service** by requiring a valid JWT token to access its API.

As you build larger microservices systems, JWTs can be extended to handle more complex scenarios such as **role-**

based access control (RBAC) or **claim-based authorization**. By securing your services in this manner, you can ensure that only authorized services and users can interact with critical components of your system, thereby improving overall security and trust.

Conclusion

In this chapter, we explored how to secure microservices communication, focusing on service-to-service authentication using **JWT**. We also discussed the concepts of **service authorization, data privacy**, and **integrating access control** in microservices. By looking at **Google's cloud security practices** and providing a hands-on tutorial, we demonstrated how to implement **JWT-based authentication** between microservices, ensuring secure communication within a distributed architecture.

With JWTs, your microservices architecture can be both **scalable** and **secure**, providing mechanisms to authenticate and authorize services while maintaining a high degree of independence between them.

CHAPTER 6: MICROSERVICES ORCHESTRATION AND KUBERNETES

In the world of microservices, managing the lifecycle of containers, automating deployments, scaling services, and ensuring reliability can quickly become overwhelming. As microservices architectures grow in complexity, the need for orchestration tools becomes evident. This chapter will dive deep into **microservices orchestration** and how tools like **Docker** and **Kubernetes** are essential in automating the deployment, scaling, and management of microservices in production environments.

We will explore the key concepts behind orchestration tools, particularly Docker and Kubernetes, and how these tools enable microservices to run smoothly at scale. Additionally, we will look at **Spotify's use of Kubernetes** to efficiently scale their microservices architecture. Finally, we'll guide you through a hands-on tutorial on setting up **Docker containers for microservices**, and we'll culminate with a project on **deploying a microservice-based application using Kubernetes**.

Key Concepts: Orchestration Tools and Containerization with Docker and Kubernetes

What is Microservices Orchestration?

In microservices, **orchestration** refers to the process of coordinating the deployment, scaling, and management of services within an environment. As the number of microservices in a system grows, managing these services manually becomes impractical. Orchestration tools provide automation and management capabilities to ensure that services are deployed consistently, scaled according to demand, and easily monitored.

Orchestration tools facilitate:

1. **Service discovery:** Finding the location of services and ensuring they can communicate with each other.

2. **Load balancing:** Distributing traffic across multiple instances of a service to ensure reliability and performance.

3. **Health checks and monitoring:** Automatically checking the health of services and restarting them when necessary.

4. **Scaling:** Automatically increasing or decreasing the number of instances of a service based on load.

At the heart of microservices orchestration is **containerization**. Containers provide a lightweight, portable way to package and deploy microservices. The two most popular tools in this ecosystem are **Docker** for containerization and **Kubernetes** for orchestration.

Docker: The Foundation of Containerization

Docker is an open-source platform that enables developers to build, ship, and run applications in containers. Containers are lightweight, isolated environments that package an application along with its dependencies, making it easy to move applications across different environments, such as development, testing, and production.

Key Features of Docker:

- **Portability:** Containers encapsulate everything an application needs to run, allowing it to run anywhere without worrying about the underlying infrastructure.

- **Efficiency:** Docker containers share the host's OS kernel, making them more efficient in terms of resources compared to virtual machines.

- **Isolation:** Containers provide a level of isolation between services, allowing each microservice to have its own runtime environment and dependencies without interfering with others.

In a microservices architecture, each service is typically packaged in its own Docker container. This allows each service to be deployed, scaled, and updated independently of the others, which aligns with the fundamental principles of microservices.

Kubernetes: The Orchestration Layer for Containers

While Docker provides the containerization platform, **Kubernetes** (often referred to as K8s) is the orchestration tool that automates the deployment, scaling, and management of containerized applications. Kubernetes is an open-source container orchestration platform originally developed by Google, and it has become the standard for managing containerized applications in production environments.

Key Features of Kubernetes:

- **Automated Deployment and Scaling:** Kubernetes automatically manages the deployment and scaling of applications. If more instances of a service are needed due to traffic, Kubernetes can scale the service up automatically.

- **Service Discovery and Load Balancing:** Kubernetes provides built-in service discovery mechanisms and can automatically balance traffic across instances of a service.

- **Self-Healing:** Kubernetes continuously monitors the health of containers. If a container or node fails, Kubernetes will automatically replace it to ensure that the application continues running smoothly.

- **Declarative Configuration:** With Kubernetes, you can declare the desired state of your application (such as the number of replicas) in a configuration file, and Kubernetes will ensure that the actual state matches the declared state.

In a microservices architecture, Kubernetes manages the lifecycle of containers across clusters of machines, handling everything from service discovery to scaling to rolling updates.

Real-World Example

Spotify, one of the world's largest music streaming platforms, is a prime example of a company that has successfully adopted Kubernetes for managing its microservices architecture. As Spotify's infrastructure grew, it faced challenges related to the complexity of managing thousands of microservices, ensuring reliable service delivery, and scaling dynamically based on traffic demands.

Spotify's Challenges Before Kubernetes

Spotify originally relied on **VMs (Virtual Machines)** to host its services, but as the number of services grew, the complexity of managing VM instances became cumbersome. Spotify also struggled with:

- **Scaling:** The need to manually adjust the number of VM instances based on changing traffic patterns.

- **Service Discovery:** Keeping track of where each service was running across multiple data centers.

- **Deployment and CI/CD:** Managing rolling updates and deployments across a large number of services.

How Spotify Solved These Challenges with Kubernetes

Spotify transitioned to **Kubernetes** to address these challenges:

- **Dynamic Scaling:** Kubernetes' ability to automatically scale the number of containers based on demand allowed Spotify to handle traffic spikes more efficiently without manual intervention.

- **Service Discovery:** Kubernetes' built-in service discovery mechanism allowed Spotify to easily track where each service was running, reducing the complexity of managing a large number of services.

- **Rolling Updates:** Kubernetes streamlined the deployment process with rolling updates, ensuring that new versions of services could be deployed without downtime.

Spotify's shift to Kubernetes enabled it to handle millions of requests per second across thousands of microservices while ensuring high availability and reliability.

Tutorial: Setting Up Docker Containers for Microservices

Now that we have a solid understanding of Docker and Kubernetes, let's walk through the process of containerizing a simple microservice using **Docker.**

In this tutorial, we'll create two microservices: a **User Service** and a **Product Service.** Both services will be containerized using Docker, which will lay the foundation for deployment in Kubernetes later.

Step 1: Setting Up the User Service

First, let's create a basic **User Service** using **Node.js** and **Express.**

1. **Create the Project Folder:**

bash

```
mkdir user-service
cd user-service
npm init -y
npm install express
```

2. **Create the server.js File:** In the user-service directory, create a server.js file:

javascript

```javascript
const express = require('express');
const app = express();
const port = 3000;

app.get('/users', (req, res) => {
  res.json([{ id: 1, name: 'John Doe' }]);
});

app.listen(port, () => {
  console.log(`User service running at
http://localhost:${port}`);
});
```

3. **Create the Dockerfile:** In the same directory, create a Dockerfile to containerize the service:

Dockerfile

```dockerfile
# Use official Node.js image from Docker Hub
FROM node:14

# Set the working directory
```

```
WORKDIR /usr/src/app

# Install dependencies
package*.json ./
RUN npm install

# the rest of the application code

. .

# Expose the port the app will run on
EXPOSE 3000

# Run the application
CMD ["node", "server.js"]
```

4. **Build and Run the Docker Container:** To build and run the Docker container, execute the following commands:

```bash
bash
```

```bash
docker build -t user-service .
docker run -p 3000:3000 user-service
```

This will start the **User Service** container on port 3000.

Step 2: Setting Up the Product Service

Next, let's create the **Product Service** following a similar process.

1. **Create the Project Folder:**

bash

```bash
mkdir product-service
cd product-service
npm init -y
npm install express
```

2. **Create the server.js File:**

javascript

```javascript
const express = require('express');
const app = express();
const port = 3001;

app.get('/products', (req, res) => {
  res.json([{ id: 1, name: 'Product A' }]);
});
```

```
app.listen(port, () => {
  console.log(`Product service running at
http://localhost:${port}`);
});
```

3. **Create the Dockerfile:** Similar to the User Service, create a Dockerfile for the Product Service:

Dockerfile

```
FROM node:14

WORKDIR /usr/src/app

package*.json ./
RUN npm install

. .

EXPOSE 3001

CMD ["node", "server.js"]
```

4. **Build and Run the Docker Container:**

bash

```
docker build -t product-service .
```

```
docker run -p 3001:3001 product-service
```

This will start the **Product Service** container on port 3001.

Project: Deploy a Microservice-Based Application Using Kubernetes

Now that we have two microservices containerized, we can deploy them using **Kubernetes**. Kubernetes provides an abstraction layer over Docker to manage containers across clusters, scale services dynamically, and handle failure recovery.

Step 1: Install Kubernetes

First, you need to have **Kubernetes** and **kubectl** installed on your machine. You can use **Minikube** to set up a local Kubernetes cluster:

bash

```
# Install Minikube (if not installed)
brew install minikube
```

```
# Start a local Kubernetes cluster
minikube start
```

Step 2: Create Kubernetes Configuration Files

Create Kubernetes deployment files for both the **User Service** and **Product Service**.

1. **User Service Deployment:** Create a file named user-service-deployment.yaml:

yaml

```yaml
apiVersion: apps/v1
kind: Deployment
metadata:
  name: user-service
spec:
  replicas: 2
  selector:
    matchLabels:
      app: user-service
  template:
```

```yaml
metadata:
  labels:
    app: user-service
spec:
  containers:
    - name: user-service
      image: user-service:latest
      ports:
        - containerPort: 3000
```

2. **Product Service Deployment:** Create a file named product-service-deployment.yaml:

yaml

```yaml
apiVersion: apps/v1
kind: Deployment
metadata:
  name: product-service
spec:
  replicas: 2
  selector:
    matchLabels:
      app: product-service
```

```
template:
  metadata:
    labels:
      app: product-service
  spec:
    containers:
      - name: product-service
        image: product-service:latest
        ports:
          - containerPort: 3001
```

Step 3: Apply Kubernetes Configurations

Now, apply the deployment files to your Kubernetes cluster using **kubectl**:

bash

```
kubectl apply -f user-service-deployment.yaml
kubectl apply -f product-service-deployment.yaml
```

Step 4: Expose Services via Kubernetes Services

To expose your services outside the Kubernetes cluster, you need to create Kubernetes services. Create user-service-service.yaml and product-service-service.yaml.

  1. **User Service Service:**

yaml

```yaml
apiVersion: v1
kind: Service
metadata:
  name: user-service
spec:
  selector:
    app: user-service
  ports:
    - protocol: TCP
      port: 80
      targetPort: 3000
  type: LoadBalancer
```

2. Product Service Service:

yaml

```yaml
apiVersion: v1
kind: Service
metadata:
  name: product-service
spec:
  selector:
    app: product-service
  ports:
    - protocol: TCP
      port: 80
      targetPort: 3001
  type: LoadBalancer
```

Apply these services with:

bash

```bash
kubectl apply -f user-service-service.yaml
kubectl apply -f product-service-service.yaml
```

Step 5: Accessing the Services

Once deployed, you can access the services via **Minikube's IP**:

bash

```
minikube service user-service
minikube service product-service
```

These commands will open the services in your default web browser.

Conclusion

In this chapter, we explored the core concepts of **microservices orchestration** and **containerization** with Docker and Kubernetes. We looked at how **Spotify** uses Kubernetes to scale its microservices efficiently and how Docker and Kubernetes can help manage complex microservices architectures.

The tutorial guided you through containerizing microservices with Docker and deploying them using Kubernetes, making your microservices scalable and manageable in production environments. By using these orchestration tools, you ensure that your microservices can scale dynamically, handle failure gracefully, and provide reliable service to users, regardless of the complexity or size of the architecture.

By mastering Docker and Kubernetes, you can confidently manage your microservices infrastructure and scale your applications to meet the demands of modern, dynamic environments.

CHAPTER 7:
MONITORING AND LOGGING IN MICROSERVICES

In a microservices architecture, the challenge of monitoring and logging becomes significantly more complex than in a monolithic system. With multiple independent services communicating with one another, ensuring that everything works as expected, identifying bottlenecks, and tracking errors can become difficult without the right tools and techniques. Therefore, robust **monitoring** and **logging** systems are vital for maintaining the health and performance of a microservices-based application.

In this chapter, we will cover the essential concepts of **distributed tracing**, **logging**, and **monitoring** within a microservices architecture. We will explore the tools commonly used in this space, including **Prometheus** for monitoring, and the **ELK stack** (Elasticsearch, Logstash, and Kibana) for logging. Additionally, we'll examine a real-world example of how **Airbnb** monitors its microservices in real-time, followed by a tutorial on setting up **centralized logging** with the ELK stack. Finally, we'll walk through a project that implements a basic **monitoring setup** for a microservices-based application.

Key Concepts

1. Distributed Tracing in Microservices

In a microservices architecture, a single user request often involves multiple services. For example, a user placing an order in an e-commerce application may trigger a cascade of calls across various services: user authentication, inventory management, payment processing, shipping, and more. Each service performs a part of the transaction, and if there is an issue—such as slow response times or errors—understanding where the problem lies can be difficult without proper tracing.

Distributed tracing provides a way to track a request across multiple services in a microservices architecture. By tagging the request with a unique trace ID, tracing systems can follow the journey of a request as it moves from one service to the next. This enables developers and operators to pinpoint which service is experiencing bottlenecks, how long each service is taking to respond, and where failures might occur.

Popular tools for distributed tracing include:

- **Jaeger**

- **Zipkin**

- **OpenTelemetry**

These tools integrate with your microservices to collect trace data and visualize it, helping you gain insights into the latency and performance of your system.

2. Centralized Logging

Logging is a critical part of monitoring microservices, but the challenge comes from the distributed nature of microservices themselves. In a traditional monolithic application, logs are often stored in a centralized location, making it easy to view and search for errors. However, in microservices, each service generates its own logs, and these logs may be scattered across multiple machines or containers. To make this process manageable, you need a **centralized logging** system that aggregates logs from all services in one place.

Centralized logging involves collecting logs from various services, systems, and containers into a central repository for easier access, search, and analysis. This is critical because without centralized logging, debugging becomes cumbersome as you need to manually access each service's logs.

Tools for centralized logging include:

- **ELK Stack (Elasticsearch, Logstash, Kibana)** – A popular open-source stack for searching, analyzing, and visualizing logs.

- **Fluentd** – A data collector that helps unify logging and works well with various logging backends.

- **Graylog** – Another open-source tool for managing and analyzing logs in real-time.

With centralized logging, logs can be enriched with metadata such as trace IDs, service names, and error codes, which makes it easier to identify issues across services.

3. Monitoring in Microservices

While logging helps capture events and errors, **monitoring** allows you to keep an eye on the health and performance of your services in real-time. Monitoring tools track metrics like CPU usage, memory consumption, request/response times, error rates, and service availability.

In microservices, **metrics** are key to understanding system performance. Monitoring systems typically gather data from services through **instrumentation**—either built-in to the application or through third-party agents—and send this data to a central location for analysis.

Prominent monitoring tools for microservices include:

- **Prometheus** – A popular open-source monitoring system designed for reliability and scalability, especially in dynamic environments like Kubernetes.

- **Grafana** – A visualization tool that integrates with Prometheus to display monitoring data in real-time dashboards.

- **Datadog** – A cloud-based monitoring and analytics platform for tracking service health and performance.

Prometheus, in particular, is highly suited for microservices because it can automatically scrape metrics from dynamically discovered services, making it ideal for environments like Kubernetes.

Real-World Example: How Airbnb Monitors Its Services in Real-Time

Airbnb operates a large and complex microservices architecture to support its online platform, which hosts millions of users, property listings, and transactions daily. Given the complexity of its system, monitoring and logging are crucial to ensure availability, detect failures, and improve performance.

Airbnb's Approach to Monitoring

Airbnb uses **Prometheus** to collect and store metrics from its microservices. The company utilizes **Grafana** for visualizing those metrics and **Alertmanager** (a component of Prometheus) to send notifications in case of service disruptions or performance degradation.

Key features of Airbnb's monitoring system include:

- **Service Health Dashboards:** Airbnb's DevOps team uses Grafana dashboards to monitor the health and performance of their services in real-time. These dashboards provide insights into response times, error rates, and resource utilization across their microservices.

- **Alerting and Incident Response:** Airbnb has set up alerts that notify engineers when services experience failures, high latency, or abnormal behavior. The company relies heavily on **alerting systems** that trigger on specific thresholds such as high error rates or request latencies, helping them address issues before they affect users.

- **Distributed Tracing:** Airbnb uses **Jaeger** for distributed tracing, allowing them to follow a user request as it travels through different services. This helps them track bottlenecks, identify slow services, and improve overall system performance.

By integrating monitoring, distributed tracing, and centralized logging, Airbnb is able to provide a seamless and reliable experience for its users, while also being proactive about detecting and resolving issues in real-time.

Tutorial: Setting Up Centralized Logging with the ELK Stack

In this tutorial, we will walk through the process of setting up a **centralized logging system** using the **ELK Stack** (Elasticsearch, Logstash, and Kibana). This setup will aggregate logs from your microservices and allow you to search, analyze, and visualize them in a central location.

Step 1: Install Elasticsearch

Elasticsearch is the search engine that powers the ELK stack. It stores logs in an index, making them easy to search and analyze.

1. **Install Elasticsearch using Docker:**

bash

```
docker pull
docker.elastic.co/elasticsearch/elasticsearch:7.10.0
docker run --name elasticsearch -d -p 9200:9200
docker.elastic.co/elasticsearch/elasticsearch:7.10.0
```

This will run Elasticsearch on your local machine at http://localhost:9200.

Step 2: Install Logstash

Logstash is the data processing pipeline that collects, parses, and forwards logs to Elasticsearch. It can collect logs from different sources (e.g., file, HTTP, Kafka) and transform them into a format Elasticsearch can index.

1. **Install Logstash using Docker:**

bash

```
docker pull docker.elastic.co/logstash/logstash:7.10.0
docker run --name logstash -d -p 5044:5044
docker.elastic.co/logstash/logstash:7.10.0
```

Step 3: Install Kibana

Kibana is the visualization layer of the ELK stack. It allows you to create dashboards and view logs in real-time.

1. **Install Kibana using Docker:**

bash

```
docker pull docker.elastic.co/kibana/kibana:7.10.0
docker run --name kibana -d -p 5601:5601
docker.elastic.co/kibana/kibana:7.10.0
```

Step 4: Configure Logstash to Collect Logs

Now that you have Elasticsearch, Logstash, and Kibana running, it's time to configure **Logstash** to collect logs from your microservices and forward them to Elasticsearch.

1. Create a file called logstash.conf with the following content:

bash

```
input {
  file {
    path => "/path/to/your/logs/*.log"
```

```
    start_position => "beginning"
  }
}
output {
  elasticsearch {
    hosts => ["http://elasticsearch:9200"]
    index => "microservices-logs-%{+YYYY.MM.dd}"
  }
}
```

This configuration tells Logstash to collect log files from a specific directory and send them to Elasticsearch, where they will be indexed under the name microservices-logs-.

Step 5: Visualizing Logs in Kibana

Once your logs are flowing into Elasticsearch via Logstash, you can visualize and analyze them using **Kibana**.

1. Open Kibana in your browser at http://localhost:5601.

2. Go to the **Discover** tab to search your logs, or go to **Dashboard** to create a custom dashboard for real-time log monitoring.

Project: Implementing a Simple Monitoring Setup for Your Microservices

Now that we have covered centralized logging, it's time to move on to monitoring. In this project, we will set up **Prometheus** and **Grafana** to monitor a simple microservices-based application.

Step 1: Install Prometheus

Prometheus is an open-source monitoring system designed for high scalability, particularly for dynamic environments like Kubernetes.

1. **Install Prometheus using Docker:**

bash

```
docker run -d -p 9090:9090 --name prometheus
prom/prometheus
```

Prometheus will now be running at http://localhost:9090.

Step 2: Install Grafana

Grafana is an open-source data visualization tool that integrates with Prometheus to display monitoring data in real-time dashboards.

1. Install Grafana using Docker:

bash

docker run -d -p 3000:3000 --name grafana grafana/grafana

Grafana will now be running at http://localhost:3000.

Step 3: Configure Prometheus to Scrape Metrics

Prometheus collects metrics from services by scraping HTTP endpoints that expose those metrics.

1. Modify the prometheus.yml configuration file to scrape metrics from your microservices. Here's a simple example:

yaml

```
scrape_configs:
  - job_name: 'microservices'
    static_configs:
      - targets: ['user-service:3000', 'product-service:3001']
```

This configuration tells Prometheus to scrape metrics from your user-service and product-service containers.

Step 4: Set Up Dashboards in Grafana

1. Open Grafana at http://localhost:3000 and configure it to use Prometheus as a data source.

2. Create a new dashboard to visualize metrics like response times, error rates, and CPU usage.

Step 5: Monitor Microservices

Once Prometheus and Grafana are set up, you can begin monitoring your microservices. You'll be able to see real-time data on metrics like:

- **Latency**: Response times for each service.

- **Throughput**: The number of requests per service.

- **Error rates**: Tracking errors in the system.

Conclusion

In this chapter, we explored the critical aspects of **monitoring and logging** in microservices, focusing on distributed tracing, centralized logging with the **ELK stack**, and the use of **Prometheus** and **Grafana** for monitoring. We examined how **Airbnb** effectively monitors its microservices, allowing it to ensure the reliability and performance of its platform.

By setting up centralized logging and monitoring, you can gain deep insights into the performance of your microservices, track down bottlenecks, and ensure that your system is reliable and scalable. The techniques and tools discussed in this chapter will help you maintain visibility over your microservices architecture and respond quickly to performance issues, making your applications more resilient and user-friendly.

CHAPTER 8:
HANDLING FAILURE
AND FAULT
TOLERANCE

Microservices architectures are designed to be flexible, scalable, and resilient, but this flexibility also introduces a significant challenge: **failure**. In a distributed system where services are independently deployed and communicate over the network, failures are inevitable. Hardware might fail, network connectivity might be interrupted, or a service might become overloaded. Handling these failures gracefully without impacting the end-user experience or causing cascading issues across the system is crucial for maintaining high availability and performance in a microservices environment.

In this chapter, we will discuss key concepts like **circuit breakers**, **retries**, and **service resilience**. We will also explore how **Amazon** ensures high availability and reliability despite service failures. Finally, we'll walk through a tutorial on **implementing a circuit breaker** with **Hystrix** and build a **resilient microservice system** that can handle failures gracefully.

Key Concepts

1. Circuit Breakers: Preventing Cascading Failures

In a distributed system, **cascading failures** can occur when a failure in one service propagates through the system, causing other dependent services to fail as well. This can lead to a complete system outage. A **circuit breaker** is a design pattern that helps prevent such cascading failures by temporarily stopping the communication with a failing service.

The circuit breaker pattern works similarly to an electrical circuit breaker: when a service encounters repeated failures or high latency, the circuit breaker "trips" and prevents further requests from being sent to that service. This allows the failing service time to recover without overloading it with requests, thus avoiding a system-wide failure.

Key States of a Circuit Breaker:

- **Closed:** The circuit is normal, and requests flow through to the service.

- **Open:** The circuit breaker is triggered, and requests to the service are blocked.

- **Half-Open:** The circuit breaker allows a limited number of requests to test if the service has recovered. If successful, the circuit breaker resets to closed; otherwise, it returns to open.

The circuit breaker pattern is often implemented using libraries such as **Hystrix**, **Resilience4j**, or **Netflix's Fallback** mechanism, allowing developers to encapsulate failure management logic and make services more resilient.

2. Retries: Increasing the Chance of Success

Sometimes, failures are temporary or caused by transient issues, such as network delays or resource contention. In these cases, **retrying** the request may allow the service to recover and succeed. **Exponential backoff** is a common approach to retries, where the delay between successive retry attempts increases exponentially. This helps to avoid overwhelming the system with retries when there is a persistent failure.

However, retries must be used cautiously. If retry attempts are made too aggressively, they can cause further load on the service, exacerbating the problem. Therefore, it is essential to implement **limits** on the number of retries, as well as **timeouts** to avoid endless retries.

3. Service Resilience: Building Fault-Tolerant Microservices

Service resilience refers to the ability of a microservice to continue functioning even in the face of failures or adverse conditions. Designing services for resilience is critical in a microservices architecture, as the failure of one service should not bring down the entire system.

Techniques for Building Resilient Microservices:

- **Timeouts:** Set appropriate timeouts for requests to prevent services from waiting indefinitely for a response.

- **Rate Limiting:** Prevent services from being overwhelmed with too many requests by implementing rate-limiting strategies.

- **Bulkheads:** Partition system resources (e.g., memory, threads) to ensure that the failure of one part of the system does not impact others.

- **Fallback Mechanisms:** When a service fails, fallback mechanisms can provide a default response, such as returning cached data or a predefined response, to ensure that the user experience is not disrupted.

By combining these techniques, microservices can tolerate and recover from failures without affecting the overall performance and availability of the system.

Real-World Example: How Amazon Handles Service Failures and Ensures High Availability

Amazon is a leading example of a company that has mastered handling failures and ensuring high availability in a microservices architecture. With its vast infrastructure supporting millions of customers globally, Amazon's architecture is designed to handle failures without causing service disruptions.

Amazon's Approach to Service Resilience

Amazon's system is designed to tolerate failures at every level. Here are some of the key techniques Amazon employs to ensure high availability:

1. **Service Isolation:** Amazon's services are isolated from one another, so a failure in one service does not impact others. If a service fails, only that service is affected, and the rest of the system continues to operate normally.

2. **Circuit Breaker Pattern:** Amazon uses circuit breakers to prevent cascading failures. If a service experiences failures, the circuit breaker is triggered, and requests to that service are stopped temporarily. This allows the service time to recover without impacting other services.

3. **Automatic Scaling:** Amazon employs automated scaling to ensure that services can handle high traffic loads. Services are automatically scaled up or down based on demand, ensuring that the system remains responsive even during traffic spikes.

4. **Retries with Exponential Backoff:** For transient failures, Amazon retries requests using exponential backoff to avoid overwhelming the system. This increases the chances of success by allowing the system time to recover between retries.

5. **Fallback Mechanisms:** In the event of a failure, Amazon uses fallback mechanisms to provide default responses to users. For instance, if a recommendation service is down, the system may show popular items instead, ensuring that the user experience is not affected.

6. **Global Redundancy:** Amazon's infrastructure is globally distributed, and services are replicated across different data centers. If one data center goes down, traffic can be rerouted to another,

ensuring that the service remains available even in the event of localized failures.

By implementing these strategies, Amazon ensures that its services are resilient and can continue to provide reliable service to its customers, even in the face of failures.

Tutorial: Implementing a Circuit Breaker with Hystrix

In this tutorial, we'll implement the **circuit breaker pattern** using **Hystrix**, a popular library from Netflix. Hystrix allows you to isolate failures, provide fallback mechanisms, and prevent cascading failures in microservices.

Step 1: Set Up a Basic Spring Boot Project

1. **Create a Spring Boot Project:**

You can create a new Spring Boot application using Spring Initializr, or use your preferred IDE to create a Spring Boot project. Make sure to include the following dependencies:

- **Spring Web**

- **Spring Boot Actuator**

- **Hystrix**

2. Add Hystrix Dependency:

In your pom.xml file, add the following dependency for Hystrix:

xml

```xml
<dependency>
  <groupId>org.springframework.cloud</groupId>
  <artifactId>spring-cloud-starter-netflix-hystrix</artifactId>
</dependency>
```

3. Enable Hystrix in Your Application:

In your main application class, enable Hystrix by adding @EnableCircuitBreaker:

java

```java
@SpringBootApplication
@EnableCircuitBreaker
public class MicroserviceApplication {
    public static void main(String[] args) {
        SpringApplication.run(MicroserviceApplication.class,
args);
    }
}
```

Step 2: Create a Service with Circuit Breaker

Let's create a simple service that simulates a failure. We'll use Hystrix to wrap the service method with a circuit breaker.

java

```java
@Service
public class ProductService {

    @HystrixCommand(fallbackMethod = "getDefaultProducts")
    public List<Product> getProducts() {
        // Simulating a failure
        if (Math.random() > 0.5) {
            throw new RuntimeException("Failed to fetch products");
        }
        return Arrays.asList(new Product("Laptop"), new Product("Phone"));
    }
```

```java
    public List<Product> getDefaultProducts() {
        return Arrays.asList(new Product("Default Laptop"),
new Product("Default Phone"));
    }
}
```

In this code:

- getProducts() is a method that simulates a failure using a random exception.

- @HystrixCommand wraps the method with a circuit breaker, and if the method fails, it will call getDefaultProducts() as a fallback.

Step 3: Create a Controller to Expose the Service

Next, create a simple controller to expose the getProducts method:

java

```java
@RestController
public class ProductController {

    @Autowired
```

```
private ProductService productService;

@GetMapping("/products")
public List<Product> getProducts() {
    return productService.getProducts();
}
}
```

Step 4: Running the Application

Now, you can run your application. When you hit the /products endpoint, if the service fails, Hystrix will trigger the fallback method (getDefaultProducts()), and you'll get a default set of products instead of an error response.

Project: Build a Resilient Microservice System That Gracefully Handles Failures

In this project, we will build a resilient **microservices system** that gracefully handles failures using the **circuit breaker** pattern, **retries**, and **fallback mechanisms**.

Step 1: Set Up Multiple Microservices

We will create two microservices: a **User Service** and a **Payment Service**. The User Service will fetch user data, and the Payment Service will handle payment transactions. If the Payment Service fails, the system will fall back to a default response.

1. **User Service:** This service will simulate fetching user data and call the Payment Service to simulate a payment request.

2. **Payment Service:** The Payment Service will simulate payment processing, with a random chance of failure. If the Payment Service fails, the User Service will use the fallback response to continue the operation.

Step 2: Implement Circuit Breakers in Both Services

Both services will use the **Hystrix** circuit breaker. In the Payment Service, we will simulate a failure, and in the User Service, we will use Hystrix to manage the failure and fall back to default values.

1. **Payment Service Circuit Breaker:**

java

```java
@Service
public class PaymentService {

    @HystrixCommand(fallbackMethod =
"fallbackProcessPayment")
    public String processPayment(String userId) {
        if (Math.random() > 0.5) {
            throw new RuntimeException("Payment processing
failed");
        }
        return "Payment processed for " + userId;
    }

    public String fallbackProcessPayment(String userId) {
        return "Default payment response for " + userId;
    }
}
```

2. **User Service Circuit Breaker:**

java

```java
@Service
public class UserService {
```

```java
@Autowired
private PaymentService paymentService;

@HystrixCommand(fallbackMethod =
"getUserDefaultPayment")
public String getUserPayment(String userId) {
    return paymentService.processPayment(userId);
}

public String getUserDefaultPayment(String userId) {
    return "User " + userId + " default payment
information";
    }
}
```

Step 3: Test the System

Run the system and test it by calling the User Service's /user/{userId}/payment endpoint. If the Payment Service fails, Hystrix will provide the fallback response, allowing the User Service to continue processing without disruption.

Conclusion

In this chapter, we explored the crucial topic of handling failure and ensuring **fault tolerance** in microservices. We discussed key concepts such as **circuit breakers, retries,** and **service resilience,** which are essential for building robust microservices architectures. Through real-world examples like **Amazon**'s approach to failure management and high availability, we learned how to design resilient systems.

We also implemented a **circuit breaker** with **Hystrix** in a hands-on tutorial and built a resilient microservice system capable of gracefully handling failures using fallback methods. By implementing these patterns and practices, you can ensure that your microservices systems remain reliable and performant, even in the face of failures.

With the knowledge of **circuit breakers, retries,** and **fallback mechanisms,** you can now build more robust and fault-tolerant systems that ensure your services continue operating smoothly even when individual components fail.

CHAPTER 9:
DEPLOYING AND SCALING MICROSERVICES

Deploying and scaling microservices is a critical part of the development lifecycle. As the number of microservices in a system grows, managing their deployment, scaling, and ensuring high availability can become complex. Effective deployment strategies and the right scaling mechanisms are necessary to ensure the system can handle high traffic, remain fault-tolerant, and deliver consistent user experiences.

In this chapter, we will cover key concepts such as **Continuous Integration/Continuous Deployment (CI/CD)** pipelines and **auto-scaling**. We will explore how **GitHub** automates its microservices deployment using pipelines, and provide a step-by-step tutorial on setting up a simple CI/CD pipeline using **Jenkins** or **GitLab**. Finally, we will walk through a project to **automate the deployment process** for a microservice-based application.

Key Concepts

1. Continuous Integration and Continuous Deployment (CI/CD)

In modern software development, **Continuous Integration (CI)** and **Continuous Deployment (CD)** are fundamental practices for ensuring that code changes are rapidly and safely integrated, tested, and deployed to production. CI/CD pipelines automate much of the process, allowing developers to push code changes with confidence, knowing that the system will automatically test, build, and deploy it.

- **Continuous Integration (CI):** The practice of continuously integrating code changes into a shared repository. Each change is automatically tested to ensure that the codebase remains stable. CI often involves running unit tests, integration tests, and static code analysis to ensure quality.

- **Continuous Deployment (CD):** The practice of automatically deploying changes to production once they have passed all tests. In the context of microservices, CD involves ensuring that individual services are updated and deployed independently without downtime.

A typical CI/CD pipeline for microservices might involve:

1. **Code Commit:** Developers push code changes to a version control system (e.g., Git).

2. **Build:** The code is automatically built and compiled.

3. **Test:** The code is tested, including unit tests, integration tests, and sometimes end-to-end tests.

4. **Deploy:** The application or service is deployed to a test/staging environment. If everything works as expected, it is automatically deployed to production.

5. **Monitor:** Once deployed, the application is monitored for errors or performance issues, ensuring that it is functioning as expected.

By automating these steps, CI/CD pipelines reduce the risk of human error, accelerate development cycles, and allow teams to quickly respond to issues.

2. Auto-Scaling Microservices

Auto-scaling is a key feature of modern microservices architectures. Since microservices are designed to scale independently, the ability to automatically scale the services based on traffic and usage is crucial for maintaining performance and reliability under changing conditions.

Auto-scaling typically involves:

- **Horizontal Scaling (Scale-out):** Adding more instances of a service to handle increased load. In Kubernetes, this is done by increasing the number of pods running a particular service.

- **Vertical Scaling (Scale-up):** Increasing the resource capacity (CPU, memory) of a single instance. This is often used for services with variable workloads or those that cannot scale horizontally.

For example, in a microservices architecture running in **Kubernetes**, the Horizontal Pod Autoscaler (HPA) automatically adjusts the number of pod replicas based on observed CPU or memory usage.

Auto-scaling helps ensure that microservices can handle varying traffic loads without human intervention, allowing businesses to remain responsive during traffic spikes while saving costs during periods of low demand.

Real-World Example: How GitHub Deploys Microservices with Automated Pipelines

GitHub, one of the world's largest and most widely-used software development platforms, uses automated CI/CD pipelines to deploy and scale its microservices. GitHub's CI/CD system enables fast and reliable deployment of microservices, allowing it to handle millions of developers using its platform every day.

GitHub's Deployment Pipeline

GitHub uses **GitHub Actions** (a feature within GitHub) as part of its deployment pipeline, along with other tools such as **Jenkins** for continuous integration. Here's a simplified flow of how GitHub deploys its microservices:

1. **Code Commit:** Developers push code to a GitHub repository. This triggers GitHub Actions to start the CI/CD pipeline.

2. **Build and Test:** The pipeline automatically builds the code and runs tests. If the tests pass, the pipeline proceeds; if not, the build fails, and the developers are notified.

3. **Staging Environment:** Once the code is built and tested, it's deployed to a **staging environment**. GitHub uses containers (typically with **Docker**) for services, making it easy to deploy and manage microservices.

4. **Production Deployment:** After successful staging, the pipeline automatically deploys the microservice to **production**. GitHub uses blue-green deployment

strategies and rolling updates to minimize downtime during deployment.

5. **Auto-scaling:** GitHub uses **Kubernetes** to scale its services up and down based on demand. Kubernetes handles service scaling and orchestration seamlessly.

By using automated pipelines, GitHub ensures that its platform can quickly deliver new features, fix bugs, and scale efficiently, without manual intervention.

Tutorial: Setting Up a Simple CI/CD Pipeline Using Jenkins or GitLab

In this tutorial, we will set up a simple CI/CD pipeline using **Jenkins** or **GitLab CI/CD**. Both Jenkins and GitLab CI are widely used CI/CD tools that automate building, testing, and deploying microservices.

Option 1: Setting Up Jenkins CI/CD Pipeline

1. **Install Jenkins:**

   o Download and install Jenkins from https://www.jenkins.io/.

   o Once installed, start Jenkins and open it in your browser at http://localhost:8080.

2. **Set Up a Jenkins Job:**

   o Create a new **Freestyle project** in Jenkins.

   o Under **Source Code Management**, choose Git and add your Git repository URL.

   o Under **Build Triggers**, select "Poll SCM" to trigger the pipeline when changes are made to the repository.

   o Under **Build**, add the steps for building and testing the code. For example:

      ▪ **Build**: Add a build step like "Execute shell" or use Docker to build the application.

      ▪ **Test**: Add a step to run unit tests or integration tests (e.g., with mvn test for a Java project).

3. **Deploy the Application:**

   o After the build and test steps, add a **Deploy** step. You can use Docker, Kubernetes, or direct deployment scripts for deploying your microservices to the appropriate environment.

4. **Automate the Pipeline:**

   o Jenkins allows you to automate the entire pipeline. Once the code is committed to the repository, Jenkins will automatically build, test, and deploy the microservice.

5. **Configure Notifications:**

   o Set up email notifications in Jenkins to alert the development team in case of build failures or issues during deployment.

Option 2: Setting Up GitLab CI/CD Pipeline

1. **Install GitLab:**

   o If you don't have a GitLab account, sign up for one at https://gitlab.com/.

   o Create a project or use an existing project to configure the CI/CD pipeline.

2. **Create a .gitlab-ci.yml File:** In the root directory of your Git repository, create a .gitlab-ci.yml file that defines the stages of the pipeline. Here is an example of a simple CI/CD pipeline configuration for a microservice:

yaml

```yaml
stages:
  - build
  - test
  - deploy

build:
  stage: build
  script:
    - docker build -t my-microservice .

test:
  stage: test
  script:
    - docker run my-microservice test

deploy:
```

```
stage: deploy

script:

 - kubectl apply -f deployment.yaml
```

In this configuration:

- o **Build Stage:** The pipeline first builds a Docker image of the microservice.

- o **Test Stage:** The pipeline runs tests on the Docker image.

- o **Deploy Stage:** The pipeline deploys the microservice to a Kubernetes cluster using the kubectl apply command.

3. **Set Up Auto-Scaling in Kubernetes:** Once the microservice is deployed using GitLab CI, you can configure **Kubernetes** to handle auto-scaling. Kubernetes uses metrics such as CPU and memory usage to scale the number of pods running a particular service. You can configure **Horizontal Pod Autoscaler** (HPA) to automatically scale services based on demand.

Project: Automating the Deployment Process for Your Microservice Application

In this project, we will build a simple CI/CD pipeline for automating the deployment of a microservice application. This pipeline will integrate Jenkins (or GitLab) to automate building, testing, and deploying microservices to a Kubernetes cluster.

Step 1: Set Up Your Microservice Application

Create a simple microservice that can be deployed to a Kubernetes cluster. For simplicity, let's use a **Node.js** application that returns a list of products.

1. **Create a Simple Node.js Application:**

bash

```
mkdir product-service
cd product-service
npm init -y
npm install express
```

In the index.js file, create a simple API:

javascript

```
const express = require('express');
const app = express();
const port = 3000;

app.get('/products', (req, res) => {
  res.json([{ id: 1, name: 'Product A' }, { id: 2, name: 'Product
B' }]);
});

app.listen(port, () => {
  console.log(`Product service running on
http://localhost:${port}`);
});
```

2. **Create a Dockerfile:**

Create a Dockerfile to containerize your microservice:

Dockerfile

FROM node:14

WORKDIR /app

package*.json ./

RUN npm install

. .

EXPOSE 3000

CMD ["node", "index.js"]

3. **Build the Docker Image:**

bash

docker build -t product-service .

Step 2: Set Up CI/CD Pipeline

Choose between **Jenkins** or **GitLab** to automate the pipeline.

1. **Using Jenkins:**

   o Set up Jenkins as described earlier to build and test your application.

   o Configure Jenkins to push the Docker image to a container registry (e.g., Docker Hub or AWS ECR).

   o Add deployment scripts to push the image to **Kubernetes**.

2. **Using GitLab:**

- o Configure the .gitlab-ci.yml file to automate the build and deployment.

- o Make sure to include the Kubernetes deployment configurations in the pipeline.

Step 3: Configure Auto-Scaling with Kubernetes

Once the service is deployed, set up auto-scaling to handle changes in traffic.

1. **Create a Horizontal Pod Autoscaler (HPA):**

yaml

```
apiVersion: apps/v1
kind: Deployment
metadata:
  name: product-service
spec:
  replicas: 2
  selector:
    matchLabels:
      app: product-service
  template:
```

```yaml
  metadata:
    labels:
      app: product-service
  spec:
    containers:
      - name: product-service
        image: product-service:latest
---
apiVersion: autoscaling/v2
kind: HorizontalPodAutoscaler
metadata:
  name: product-service
spec:
  scaleTargetRef:
    apiVersion: apps/v1
    kind: Deployment
    name: product-service
  minReplicas: 2
  maxReplicas: 10
  metrics:
  - type: Resource
    resource:
```

```
name: cpu
target:
 type: Utilization
 averageUtilization: 50
```

This HPA configuration will automatically scale the number of pods between 2 and 10 based on CPU utilization.

Step 4: Test the System

Once the pipeline is set up, push changes to your Git repository and watch the automation kick in:

1. Jenkins or GitLab will build and test the microservice.

2. The new Docker image will be deployed to your Kubernetes cluster.

3. Kubernetes will handle auto-scaling based on demand.

Conclusion

In this chapter, we explored how to automate the deployment and scaling of microservices using **CI/CD pipelines** and **auto-scaling** techniques. We looked at real-world examples like **GitHub** and **Amazon**, which rely on automated pipelines to streamline deployments and ensure high availability. We also provided a hands-on tutorial on setting up a simple CI/CD pipeline using **Jenkins** or **GitLab** and walked through a project that automates the deployment process of a microservice application.

By adopting **CI/CD pipelines** and **auto-scaling**, you can ensure that your microservices are deployed efficiently, can handle varying levels of traffic, and remain highly available and resilient to failures. This approach accelerates development cycles, reduces human error, and enables your applications to scale seamlessly in production environments.

CHAPTER 10: REAL-WORLD APPLICATION: BUILDING A SCALABLE E-COMMERCE PLATFORM

In this chapter, we will apply all the concepts we've covered in previous chapters to create a real-world **scalable e-commerce platform** using a **microservices architecture**. This project will demonstrate how to build an entire platform consisting of multiple microservices that can scale independently. We'll cover everything from designing the services to deploying and scaling the system in production.

Key Concepts

Building a scalable and efficient e-commerce platform using **microservices** requires an understanding of how to integrate various system components, each of which might be independently deployable, scalable, and resilient. Here are the key concepts we'll be using throughout this project:

1. **Microservices Architecture:** We will break down the e-commerce platform into separate services such as Product, Order, and User services. Each service will handle a distinct set of responsibilities and be deployable independently.

2. **Service Discovery and Communication:** These microservices will communicate with each other using APIs. We'll implement **synchronous** (REST) and **asynchronous** (message queues) communication where necessary.

3. **Resilience and Fault Tolerance:** We will implement **circuit breakers**, retries, and fallback mechanisms to ensure the system is fault-tolerant. This will allow the platform to handle failures gracefully and maintain high availability.

4. **Scalability:** We'll deploy the platform on a containerized infrastructure using **Docker** and **Kubernetes**. Kubernetes will handle auto-scaling, ensuring that the platform can scale based on traffic.

5. **CI/CD Pipelines:** We will integrate **CI/CD pipelines** to automate the deployment process, enabling

rapid iteration and deployment of new features or fixes.

6. **Logging and Monitoring:** We will set up centralized logging and monitoring to track the health of the platform and quickly identify and resolve issues.

By the end of this chapter, we'll have implemented a complete, scalable e-commerce platform with microservices that can handle real-world traffic loads.

Real-World Example: How an E-Commerce Platform Like Amazon Can Scale with Microservices

Amazon is one of the most popular examples of an e-commerce platform that utilizes microservices to scale its operations efficiently. Amazon's platform is vast and highly complex, with millions of users, product listings, and transactions happening every second. Here's how Amazon scales its platform with microservices:

1. **Microservices-Based Architecture:** Amazon's platform is built using a microservices architecture, where each core functionality (e.g., user management, product listings, payments) is handled by an independent service.

2. **Service Communication:** Services communicate using **RESTful APIs** for synchronous operations and **message queues** for asynchronous tasks like order processing, inventory updates, and shipping notifications.

3. **Scalability and Resilience:** Amazon uses **Kubernetes** for container orchestration, allowing it to automatically scale services based on demand. It employs techniques like **auto-scaling** and **load balancing** to distribute traffic and prevent overloads.

4. **CI/CD and Automation:** Amazon uses automated pipelines to deploy and test updates to individual services independently, ensuring that the platform remains up-to-date without downtime.

5. **Monitoring and Observability:** Amazon monitors its services using tools like **Prometheus** and **Grafana**, which provide insights into the performance and health of each microservice.

This architecture allows Amazon to handle millions of users and transactions in real time while providing a seamless user experience. In our project, we'll replicate a simplified version of this architecture for our e-commerce platform.

Tutorial: Building an E-Commerce Platform with Multiple Microservices (Product, Order, and User)

In this tutorial, we will create an e-commerce platform with three primary microservices:

- **Product Service:** Manages product listings and details.

- **Order Service:** Handles user orders, payment processing, and order status.

- **User Service:** Manages user profiles, authentication, and authorization.

We'll use **Spring Boot** for creating microservices, **Docker** for containerization, and **Kubernetes** for orchestration and auto-scaling.

Step 1: Setting Up the Product Service

The **Product Service** will be responsible for storing and retrieving product information. It will expose a REST API for interacting with product data.

1. **Initialize the Spring Boot Project for Product Service:**

Create a new **Spring Boot** project with the following dependencies:

- **Spring Web** (for creating REST APIs)

- **Spring Data JPA** (for interacting with a relational database)

- **H2 Database** (for simplicity, we will use an in-memory database)

2. **Define the Product Entity:**

In ProductService/src/main/java/com/example/products/ create a Product class.

java

```java
@Entity
public class Product {

    @Id
    @GeneratedValue(strategy = GenerationType.IDENTITY)
    private Long id;

    private String name;
```

```java
private String description;
private Double price;

// Getters and setters omitted for brevity
}
```

3. Create the Product Repository:

In ProductService/src/main/java/com/example/products/ create a ProductRepository interface.

java

```java
public interface ProductRepository extends
JpaRepository<Product, Long> {
    List<Product> findByNameContaining(String name);
}
```

4. Create the Product Controller:

In ProductService/src/main/java/com/example/products/ create a ProductController class to handle HTTP requests.

java

```java
@RestController
@RequestMapping("/products")
public class ProductController {
```

```java
@Autowired
private ProductRepository productRepository;

@GetMapping
public List<Product> getAllProducts() {
    return productRepository.findAll();
}

@GetMapping("/{id}")
public Product getProductById(@PathVariable Long id) {
    return productRepository.findById(id).orElseThrow(() -> new ProductNotFoundException(id));
}
}
```

5. **Dockerize the Product Service:**

Create a Dockerfile in the ProductService directory.

Dockerfile

```
FROM openjdk:11-jre-slim
WORKDIR /app
target/product-service.jar product-service.jar
```

```
CMD ["java", "-jar", "product-service.jar"]
EXPOSE 8080
```

Build the Docker image:

```bash
```

```
docker build -t product-service .
```

Step 2: Setting Up the Order Service

The **Order Service** will manage customer orders, including placing new orders, processing payments, and updating the order status.

1. **Initialize the Spring Boot Project for Order Service:**

Follow the same steps as the Product Service, but this time create an **Order Service** project. This project will also include dependencies for **Spring Web, Spring Data JPA,** and a **MySQL Database.**

2. **Define the Order Entity:**

In OrderService/src/main/java/com/example/orders/ create an Order class.

```java
```

```java
@Entity
public class Order {

    @Id
    @GeneratedValue(strategy = GenerationType.IDENTITY)
    private Long id;

    private Long productId;
    private Long userId;
    private String status;

    // Getters and setters omitted for brevity
}
```

3. **Create the Order Repository:**

java

```java
public interface OrderRepository extends
JpaRepository<Order, Long> {
    List<Order> findByUserId(Long userId);
}
```

4. **Create the Order Controller:**

java

```java
@RestController
@RequestMapping("/orders")
public class OrderController {

    @Autowired
    private OrderRepository orderRepository;

    @PostMapping
    public Order createOrder(@RequestBody Order order) {
        return orderRepository.save(order);
    }

    @GetMapping("/{userId}")
    public List<Order> getOrdersByUser(@PathVariable Long userId) {
        return orderRepository.findByUserId(userId);
    }
}
```

5. Dockerize the Order Service:

Create a Dockerfile for the Order Service, similar to the Product Service.

Dockerfile

```
FROM openjdk:11-jre-slim
WORKDIR /app
target/order-service.jar order-service.jar
CMD ["java", "-jar", "order-service.jar"]
EXPOSE 8080
```

Build the Docker image:

bash

```
docker build -t order-service .
```

Step 3: Setting Up the User Service

The **User Service** will manage user authentication, profile information, and order history.

1. **Initialize the Spring Boot Project for User Service:**

Create a **User Service** project with dependencies for **Spring Web, Spring Security, Spring Data JPA**, and **JWT (JSON Web Token)** for authentication.

2. Define the User Entity:

java

```java
@Entity
public class User {

    @Id
    @GeneratedValue(strategy = GenerationType.IDENTITY)
    private Long id;

    private String username;
    private String password;

    // Getters and setters omitted for brevity
}
```

3. Create the User Repository:

java

```java
public interface UserRepository extends JpaRepository<User, Long> {
    Optional<User> findByUsername(String username);
}
```

4. Create the User Controller:

java

```java
@RestController
@RequestMapping("/users")
public class UserController {

    @Autowired
    private UserRepository userRepository;

    @PostMapping("/register")
    public User registerUser(@RequestBody User user) {
        return userRepository.save(user);
    }

    @PostMapping("/login")
    public String loginUser(@RequestBody User user) {
        // Validate user credentials and generate JWT token
        return "JWT Token";
    }
}
```

5. **Dockerize the User Service:**

Create a Dockerfile for the User Service:

Dockerfile

```
FROM openjdk:11-jre-slim
WORKDIR /app
target/user-service.jar user-service.jar
CMD ["java", "-jar", "user-service.jar"]
EXPOSE 8080
```

Build the Docker image:

bash

```
docker build -t user-service .
```

Step 4: Deploying and Scaling the Microservices with Kubernetes

Now that we have our three microservices, we need to deploy them to a scalable environment using **Kubernetes**. We will use **Docker** containers and Kubernetes to manage and scale our microservices.

1. Kubernetes Setup:

Create a Kubernetes cluster using a cloud provider (e.g., AWS, Google Cloud, or Azure) or locally using **Minikube**.

2. Kubernetes Deployment Files:

For each microservice, create a Kubernetes deployment file that defines how the microservice should be deployed, scaled, and exposed.

1. **Product Service Deployment:**

yaml

```yaml
apiVersion: apps/v1
kind: Deployment
metadata:
  name: product-service
spec:
  replicas: 3
  selector:
    matchLabels:
      app: product-service
  template:
    metadata:
      labels:
```

```
    app: product-service
  spec:
    containers:
      - name: product-service
        image: product-service:latest
        ports:
          - containerPort: 8080
```

2. **Order Service Deployment:**

yaml

```
apiVersion: apps/v1
kind: Deployment
metadata:
  name: order-service
spec:
  replicas: 3
  selector:
    matchLabels:
      app: order-service
  template:
    metadata:
      labels:
```

```yaml
      app: order-service
  spec:
    containers:
      - name: order-service
        image: order-service:latest
        ports:
          - containerPort: 8080
```

3. **User Service Deployment:**

yaml

```yaml
apiVersion: apps/v1
kind: Deployment
metadata:
  name: user-service
spec:
  replicas: 3
  selector:
    matchLabels:
      app: user-service
  template:
    metadata:
      labels:
```

```yaml
    app: user-service
  spec:
    containers:
      - name: user-service
        image: user-service:latest
        ports:
          - containerPort: 8080
```

3. Kubernetes Services:

Create Kubernetes services to expose each microservice to the network.

1. Product Service Service:

yaml

```yaml
apiVersion: v1
kind: Service
metadata:
  name: product-service
spec:
  selector:
    app: product-service
  ports:
    - protocol: TCP
```

```
    port: 8080
    targetPort: 8080
```

2. **Order Service Service:**

yaml

```
apiVersion: v1
kind: Service
metadata:
  name: order-service
spec:
  selector:
    app: order-service
  ports:
    - protocol: TCP
      port: 8080
      targetPort: 8080
```

3. **User Service Service:**

yaml

```
apiVersion: v1
kind: Service
metadata:
```

```yaml
  name: user-service
spec:
  selector:
    app: user-service
  ports:
    - protocol: TCP
      port: 8080
      targetPort: 8080
```

4. Auto-scaling with Kubernetes:

Use the **Horizontal Pod Autoscaler (HPA)** to automatically scale the number of replicas based on CPU usage or other metrics.

yaml

```yaml
apiVersion: autoscaling/v2
kind: HorizontalPodAutoscaler
metadata:
  name: product-service
spec:
  scaleTargetRef:
    apiVersion: apps/v1
    kind: Deployment
```

```
name: product-service
minReplicas: 2
maxReplicas: 10
metrics:
- type: Resource
  resource:
    name: cpu
    target:
      type: Utilization
      averageUtilization: 50
```

Step 5: Test and Monitor the E-Commerce Platform

1. Test the Platform:

After deploying the microservices and configuring auto-scaling, access the platform by sending requests to the exposed services. Use **Postman** or **cURL** to test the product, order, and user services.

2. Monitor the Services:

Use **Prometheus** and **Grafana** for monitoring the health of your services. Set up dashboards in Grafana to visualize metrics like CPU usage, memory consumption, and request/response times.

Conclusion

In this chapter, we demonstrated how to build a **scalable e-commerce platform** using a **microservices architecture**. By breaking down the platform into **Product**, **Order**, and **User** services, we created a system that can scale independently based on demand. We used **Docker** for containerization, **Kubernetes** for orchestration and auto-scaling, and **CI/CD pipelines** for automated deployment.

The architecture we built is highly resilient, with each microservice deployed independently, able to scale automatically based on traffic, and equipped with monitoring and logging for proactive issue detection. By applying the principles learned throughout this book, we've created a real-world application that can handle high traffic, ensure fault tolerance, and deliver a seamless user experience.

CHAPTER 11:
ADVANCED SERVICE DISCOVERY AND LOAD BALANCING

In large-scale microservices architectures, service discovery and load balancing are critical to ensuring that services can efficiently and reliably communicate with each other. These mechanisms are crucial when scaling applications, managing distributed systems, and maintaining high availability. As the number of services grows, manually managing service communication becomes cumbersome, which is why automated service discovery and dynamic load balancing are integral to modern systems.

In this chapter, we will delve into **service discovery mechanisms**, **dynamic load balancing**, and **health checks**. We will also explore a **real-world example** of how **Kubernetes** uses service discovery to manage traffic, followed by a hands-on tutorial on setting up **service discovery with Consul**. Lastly, we will implement **load balancing** for a set of microservices to optimize traffic distribution and ensure fault tolerance.

Key Concepts

1. Service Discovery Mechanisms

In a microservices architecture, services often need to communicate with one another. For example, a **User Service** might need to communicate with an **Order Service** or a **Payment Service**. However, the location of these services might change frequently, especially when scaling up or down, or when services are running on dynamic infrastructure such as **Kubernetes** or cloud-based environments.

Service discovery is the process by which a service can automatically find and communicate with other services within the system. It eliminates the need for hardcoded IP addresses or static configurations, enabling services to dynamically discover each other as they scale or as the infrastructure changes.

There are two main approaches to service discovery:

1. **Client-Side Discovery:** The client (consumer) of a service is responsible for determining the location of the service and routing the requests accordingly. The client queries a **service registry** (such as

Consul, Eureka, or **Zookeeper**) to discover the available instances of a service.

2. **Server-Side Discovery:** The client sends requests to a **load balancer** or **API gateway**, which is responsible for querying the service registry and routing the requests to the appropriate service instance. In this model, the load balancer handles service discovery on behalf of the client.

In both approaches, services register themselves with a **service registry** when they start up and deregister when they shut down. The registry keeps track of the available instances and their corresponding metadata (e.g., host, port, health status). Popular tools for service discovery include **Consul, Eureka**, and **Kubernetes DNS**.

2. Dynamic Load Balancing

Once services discover each other, **load balancing** comes into play. Load balancing ensures that requests are evenly distributed among available instances of a service to avoid overloading any single instance and to improve fault tolerance. Load balancing can be categorized into **static** and **dynamic** load balancing.

- **Static Load Balancing:** In static load balancing, traffic is routed to a fixed set of servers based on predetermined configurations, such as round-robin or least connections. While this approach works for small, stable systems, it lacks flexibility when scaling services or handling dynamic changes in the network.

- **Dynamic Load Balancing:** In dynamic load balancing, traffic is distributed based on real-time metrics such as response time, request rate, or system health. Dynamic load balancers can adjust the distribution of traffic as services are added or removed from the system, ensuring that the load is always balanced optimally.

In modern systems, dynamic load balancing is typically implemented using **service discovery** combined with **health checks**, so the load balancer knows which services are healthy and capable of handling traffic.

Common tools for load balancing include:

- **Nginx** and **HAProxy** for reverse proxy and load balancing.

- **Kubernetes Ingress** controllers that manage traffic routing and load balancing.

- **Envoy** and **Traefik** for service mesh environments.

3. Health Checks

To ensure that the services receiving traffic are healthy and operational, **health checks** are implemented. Health checks allow load balancers or service discovery tools to determine whether a service is able to handle traffic. If a service instance fails its health check, it will be removed from the load balancer's pool of available instances until it recovers.

Health checks generally fall into two types:

1. **Liveness Checks:** These checks determine if the service is running and responsive. If the service fails the liveness check, it may be restarted.

2. **Readiness Checks:** These checks verify if the service is ready to handle traffic. If a service fails the readiness check, it is temporarily removed from the load balancing pool, allowing traffic to be routed to other instances.

Health checks are typically exposed via HTTP endpoints (e.g., /health), or can be integrated into the container orchestration system like **Kubernetes** to automatically manage the health of microservices.

Real-World Example: How Kubernetes Uses Service Discovery to Manage Traffic

Kubernetes is a powerful container orchestration tool that simplifies the management of microservices architectures. It offers built-in **service discovery** and **load balancing** features to ensure seamless communication between services and optimal traffic distribution.

Kubernetes Service Discovery

In Kubernetes, **services** are abstractions that define a logical set of Pods (containers) and provide stable access to them, regardless of the individual Pods' IP addresses. Kubernetes uses a DNS-based service discovery mechanism to allow one service to find and communicate with another.

1. **Service Definition:** Each service in Kubernetes is defined by a **Service** resource, which provides a stable DNS name (e.g., product-service.default.svc.cluster.local) and an IP address that can be used to access the service.

2. **Automatic Discovery:** When a pod is created, Kubernetes automatically registers it with the DNS service. For example, if a **Product Service** is exposed via a Kubernetes service named product-

service, other services within the cluster can communicate with it by referring to the product-service DNS name.

3. **Load Balancing:** Kubernetes uses **Endpoints** associated with a service to keep track of the Pods that are part of the service. When a request is made to a service, Kubernetes automatically load balances the traffic across the available Pods based on the service's configuration.

4. **Health Checks and Auto-Healing:** Kubernetes continuously monitors the health of Pods using **readiness** and **liveness probes**. If a Pod fails the readiness check, it is removed from the load balancer pool until it is ready again. If a Pod fails the liveness check, Kubernetes will automatically restart it.

Kubernetes combines service discovery with dynamic load balancing and health checks to manage traffic and ensure high availability and fault tolerance across microservices.

Tutorial: Setting Up Service Discovery with Consul

In this tutorial, we'll set up **service discovery** with **Consul**, a tool from HashiCorp that provides service discovery, health checking, and key-value storage. We'll implement service discovery for two microservices: **Product Service** and **Order Service.**

Step 1: Install Consul

First, we need to install **Consul** on our machine or in a container. To run Consul in a Docker container:

bash

```
docker run -d --name consul -p 8500:8500 consul:latest
```

This command runs Consul in the background and exposes the web UI on http://localhost:8500.

Step 2: Register Services with Consul

1. **Product Service:** For the **Product Service**, we will configure Consul to register the service. First, create a configuration file for the service registration. Create a file named product-service.json:

json

```
{
  "service": {
    "name": "product-service",
    "tags": ["api", "product"],
```

```json
    "port": 8081,
    "check": {
      "http": "http://localhost:8081/health",
      "interval": "10s"
    }
  }
}
```

2. **Order Service:** Similarly, create a configuration file for the **Order Service**. Create a file named order-service.json:

json

```json
{
  "service": {
    "name": "order-service",
    "tags": ["api", "order"],
    "port": 8082,
    "check": {
      "http": "http://localhost:8082/health",
      "interval": "10s"
    }
  }
}
```

Step 3: Configure Service Registration with Consul

Now, we need to register both services with Consul. To do this, we'll start Consul agent with the following command:

bash

```
docker exec -it consul consul agent -dev -config-
dir=/consul/config
```

Next, register the **Product Service** and **Order Service** by using Consul's CLI or HTTP API. You can do this manually with the following command:

bash

```
curl --request PUT --data @product-service.json
http://localhost:8500/v1/agent/service/register
curl --request PUT --data @order-service.json
http://localhost:8500/v1/agent/service/register
```

Step 4: Service Discovery with Consul API

To discover the services, you can use the Consul HTTP API to query the available services. For example:

bash

```
curl http://localhost:8500/v1/catalog/service/product-service
```

```
curl http://localhost:8500/v1/catalog/service/order-service
```

These requests will return the list of service instances registered with Consul, along with their IPs and ports.

Project: Implementing Load Balancing for a Set of Microservices

Now that we have set up service discovery with **Consul**, it's time to implement **dynamic load balancing** for our microservices. We'll use **HAProxy** as the load balancer to distribute traffic across the available instances of the services.

Step 1: Set Up HAProxy for Load Balancing

1. **Install HAProxy:** On your machine, install **HAProxy**:

bash

```bash
sudo apt-get install haproxy
```

2. **Configure HAProxy:** Create a haproxy.cfg file to configure load balancing for the Product and Order services:

haproxy

```
global
    log /dev/log local0
    maxconn 200

defaults
    log     global
    option  httplog
    option  dontlognull
    timeout connect 5000ms
    timeout client  50000ms
    timeout server  50000ms

frontend http_front
    bind *:80
    acl is_product_service hdr(host) -i product-service.local
    acl is_order_service hdr(host) -i order-service.local
    use_backend product_backend if is_product_service
    use_backend order_backend if is_order_service
```

```
backend product_backend

    server product1 127.0.0.1:8081 check

    server product2 127.0.0.1:8083 check


backend order_backend

    server order1 127.0.0.1:8082 check

    server order2 127.0.0.1:8084 check
```

In this configuration:

- Traffic to product-service.local is routed to the product_backend, which load balances between product1 and product2.

- Traffic to order-service.local is routed to the order_backend, which load balances between order1 and order2.

Step 2: Test Load Balancing

1. **Start Your Microservices:** Make sure you have multiple instances of your **Product Service** and **Order Service** running on different ports. You can start multiple containers or use different ports on the same machine.

2. **Start HAProxy:** Start HAProxy with the following command:

bash

```
sudo haproxy -f /path/to/haproxy.cfg
```

3. **Access the Services:** Test load balancing by accessing the services through http://product-service.local and http://order-service.local. HAProxy will route the traffic to the available instances of each service.

Conclusion

In this chapter, we explored **advanced service discovery**, **dynamic load balancing**, and **health checks**, which are essential for managing traffic and ensuring the reliability of microservices-based architectures. We also demonstrated how **Kubernetes** uses service discovery to manage traffic and how to set up service discovery with **Consul**.

Through the **load balancing** project, we implemented HAProxy to dynamically distribute traffic across multiple instances of microservices, ensuring that the system can handle high traffic loads and recover from failures. By using **Consul** for service discovery, **HAProxy** for load balancing, and **health checks** for monitoring service health, we created a scalable, resilient architecture capable of handling the demands of modern distributed systems.

By integrating service discovery, load balancing, and health checks, you ensure that your microservices system remains performant, fault-tolerant, and scalable, allowing it to handle real-world traffic while maintaining reliability and uptime.

CHAPTER 12: INTEGRATING WITH EXTERNAL APIS

In modern microservices architectures, integrating with external APIs is a crucial part of building flexible, feature-rich applications. Whether it's for **payments**, **notifications**, or **data services**, external APIs provide powerful functionalities that microservices can leverage without reinventing the wheel. As the ecosystem of third-party services grows, microservices must be capable of seamlessly communicating with external systems, ensuring scalability, fault tolerance, and performance.

In this chapter, we will cover the key concepts around how microservices can communicate with third-party APIs, including **authentication**, **rate limiting**, and **error handling**. We will examine a **real-world example** of how **Twitter** integrates various third-party services and explore a **tutorial** on connecting a microservice to an external **payment gateway API**. Lastly, we will walk through a **project** where we will integrate a third-party API (for either **payments** or **email services**) into a microservice-based application.

Key Concept

1. Communication with External APIs

Microservices communicate with third-party APIs through **HTTP-based protocols** such as **RESTful** APIs or **GraphQL** APIs. The core of these integrations lies in managing the communication between your microservices and the external system, ensuring that your services remain decoupled, scalable, and resilient.

The communication with external APIs often involves the following components:

1. **HTTP Methods:** Microservices communicate with external APIs using standard HTTP methods like GET, POST, PUT, DELETE, or PATCH. The method used depends on the operation the external API supports.

2. **Authentication and Authorization:** Most third-party APIs require authentication, either using **API keys**, **OAuth tokens**, or other methods. This ensures that only authorized systems can make requests to the API. Secure handling of credentials and tokens is essential.

3. **Rate Limiting and Throttling:** Many third-party APIs have **rate limits** to prevent abuse. For instance, an API might allow only 1000 requests per minute.

Microservices should be able to handle rate limiting gracefully, using techniques like **caching, retry mechanisms,** or **backoff strategies.**

4. **Error Handling:** External APIs can fail for various reasons, such as network issues, service downtime, or invalid data. Proper error handling ensures that failures in the external API don't impact the core functionality of the microservices.

5. **Serialization and Deserialization:** When microservices send requests to or receive responses from third-party APIs, they need to serialize data into a format that the API understands (such as **JSON** or **XML**). Similarly, the response data needs to be deserialized into a usable format.

2. Authentication and Security

When integrating third-party services into a microservices architecture, handling authentication securely is essential. Here are a few approaches:

1. **API Keys:** API keys are a common form of authentication where the third-party service provides a unique key that the microservice includes in its HTTP request headers.

2. **OAuth:** Many APIs (such as Google, Twitter, and GitHub) use OAuth authentication. OAuth allows

microservices to obtain a token on behalf of a user, which is used to authenticate requests.

3. **JWT (JSON Web Tokens):** For APIs requiring user-based authentication, **JWT tokens** can be used for stateless authentication. These tokens contain claims about the user and can be passed in API requests.

3. Rate Limiting and Throttling

Third-party services typically implement **rate limiting** to protect themselves from overuse or abuse. If you exceed the allowed number of requests within a specified time frame, the service will return a rate-limiting error, often with a message indicating when you can retry.

Microservices should handle this gracefully by:

- **Caching Responses:** Storing data locally to avoid redundant requests to external APIs.

- **Exponential Backoff:** Introducing a delay before retrying requests to avoid overwhelming the service.

4. Handling Failures and Retries

When a microservice relies on external APIs, it's essential to build **resilience** into the system. This involves:

- **Circuit Breaker Pattern:** If a third-party API becomes unavailable, the circuit breaker prevents the system from making further requests, allowing the external system time to recover.

- **Retries:** If the external API is temporarily unavailable, microservices can use a retry mechanism with **exponential backoff**.

- **Fallbacks:** In case of failure, fallback mechanisms should provide default or cached responses.

5. Monitoring and Logging

Microservices should log their interactions with third-party APIs, capturing details such as request URLs, response times, status codes, and any errors that occur. Monitoring tools like **Prometheus**, **Grafana**, or **Elasticsearch** can help track the health of these integrations and alert the team in case of issues.

Real-World Example: How Twitter Integrates Various Third-Party Services

Twitter, one of the world's largest social media platforms, leverages multiple external APIs to enhance its functionality. From **payment gateways** to **email notifications** and **analytics services**, Twitter's system integrates with many third-party APIs to deliver seamless user experiences.

1. Payment Gateway Integration

Twitter uses third-party APIs to process payments for premium services like Twitter Ads or Twitter Blue (a subscription service). These payment APIs handle everything from **user authentication** and **transaction processing** to **fraud prevention** and **invoice generation**.

2. Email Services

Twitter integrates with external email services like **SendGrid** or **Amazon SES** to send verification emails, notifications, or password resets. These services allow Twitter to scale its email infrastructure without needing to manage the complexity of building and maintaining its own email delivery system.

3. Analytics and Monitoring

Twitter also uses third-party analytics services like **Google Analytics** or **Mixpanel** to track user behavior, engagement, and performance metrics. This allows Twitter to gather insights into user interactions and optimize the platform accordingly.

How Twitter Manages These Integrations

To handle these external dependencies, Twitter employs best practices for API integration:

1. **Authentication:** APIs are securely authenticated using OAuth tokens or API keys, with tokens refreshed periodically.

2. **Rate Limiting:** Twitter's system implements rate limiting and ensures requests are made within the API's rate limits using a combination of caching and backoff strategies.

3. **Resilience:** Twitter uses **circuit breakers** to handle failures from external services and **caching** to reduce unnecessary external calls.

These techniques ensure that Twitter can continue to provide high availability and a seamless user experience, even when relying on third-party services.

Tutorial: Connecting Your Microservices to an External API (e.g., Payment Gateway API)

In this tutorial, we will connect a microservice to a **payment gateway API** to process payments for an e-commerce application. We'll use the **Stripe API** as an example, which is a widely used payment processing service.

Step 1: Set Up the Payment Service

1. **Create a Spring Boot Project for Payment Service:**

Generate a new Spring Boot project with the following dependencies:

- **Spring Web**

- **Spring Boot Starter for REST**

- **Stripe SDK** (for integrating with the Stripe API)

2. **Configure Stripe API Keys:**

In your application.properties file, add the Stripe API keys:

properties

```
stripe.api.key=your_secret_key_here
```

Step 2: Integrating Stripe Payment API

1. Create the Payment Controller:

In the PaymentService/src/main/java/com/example/payment/ directory, create a PaymentController class:

java

```java
@RestController
@RequestMapping("/payments")
public class PaymentController {

  @Value("${stripe.api.key}")
  private String stripeApiKey;

  @PostMapping("/charge")
  public ResponseEntity<String> charge(@RequestBody PaymentRequest paymentRequest) {
    try {
      // Set the Stripe API key
      Stripe.apiKey = stripeApiKey;

      // Create a charge
```

```java
        Map<String, Object> chargeParams = new
HashMap<>();
        chargeParams.put("amount",
paymentRequest.getAmount());
        chargeParams.put("currency", "usd");
        chargeParams.put("source",
paymentRequest.getToken()); // Token is generated on the
client side
        Charge charge = Charge.create(chargeParams);

        // Return success response
        return ResponseEntity.ok("Payment successful.
Charge ID: " + charge.getId());
    } catch (StripeException e) {
        // Handle errors
        return
ResponseEntity.status(HttpStatus.BAD_REQUEST).body("P
ayment failed: " + e.getMessage());
    }
  }
}
```

In this controller, we use the **Stripe API** to charge a customer. The payment request contains the amount and token (generated from the client side). If successful, the charge ID is returned.

2. **Define the PaymentRequest Class:**

java

```
public class PaymentRequest {

    private Integer amount;
    private String token;

    // Getters and setters omitted for brevity
}
```

Step 3: Testing the Payment Service

Once the Payment Service is set up, you can test it by sending a **POST request** to /payments/charge with the payment details.

You can use **Postman** or any HTTP client to send a request:

bash

POST http://localhost:8080/payments/charge

Content-Type: application/json

```
{

    "amount": 5000,

    "token": "tok_visa"

}
```

In response, you should receive a confirmation that the payment was successfully processed.

Project: Integrate a Third-Party API into Your Application to Handle Payments or Emails

In this project, we will integrate **SendGrid** (an email service) into our microservices system to handle transactional emails. We will use the following steps:

Step 1: Set Up SendGrid API

1. **Create a SendGrid Account:**

Go to SendGrid and sign up for an account. After signing up, generate an API key to send emails.

2. Add SendGrid API Key to the Microservice:

In your application.properties file, add the following properties:

properties

sendgrid.api.key=your_sendgrid_api_key

Step 2: Create the Email Service

In EmailService/src/main/java/com/example/email/ create an EmailService class that will send emails via the SendGrid API.

1. Create the EmailService Class:

java

```java
@Service
public class EmailService {

    @Value("${sendgrid.api.key}")
    private String sendGridApiKey;

    public String sendEmail(String recipientEmail, String
subject, String body) {
```

```
try {
    Email from = new Email("no-reply@myapp.com");
    Email to = new Email(recipientEmail);
    Content content = new Content("text/plain", body);
    Mail mail = new Mail(from, subject, to, content);

    SendGrid sg = new SendGrid(sendGridApiKey);
    Request request = new Request();
    request.setMethod(Method.POST);
    request.setEndpoint("mail/send");
    request.setBody(mail.build());

    sg.api(request);
    return "Email sent successfully.";
} catch (IOException ex) {
    return "Error sending email: " + ex.getMessage();
}
    }
}
```

This service uses the **SendGrid API** to send an email. The sendEmail() method creates a Mail object with the subject and body of the email and sends it via the SendGrid API.

2. Create the Email Controller:

java

```java
@RestController
@RequestMapping("/emails")
public class EmailController {

    @Autowired
    private EmailService emailService;

    @PostMapping("/send")
    public ResponseEntity<String> sendEmail(@RequestBody
EmailRequest emailRequest) {
        String response =
emailService.sendEmail(emailRequest.getRecipientEmail(),
emailRequest.getSubject(), emailRequest.getBody());
        return ResponseEntity.ok(response);
    }
}
```

3. Define the EmailRequest Class:

java

```java
public class EmailRequest {

    private String recipientEmail;
    private String subject;
    private String body;

    // Getters and setters omitted for brevity
}
```

Step 3: Test the Email Service

Now that the email service is set up, you can test it by sending a POST request to /emails/send with the following JSON payload:

json

```json
{
    "recipientEmail": "user@example.com",
    "subject": "Welcome to Our Service",
    "body": "Thank you for signing up!"
```

}

If everything is configured correctly, you should receive a confirmation that the email was sent successfully.

Conclusion

In this chapter, we explored how to integrate external third-party APIs into microservices, focusing on **payment gateway integration** and **email service integration**. We covered key concepts such as **authentication, rate limiting, error handling**, and **service resilience**.

By building a payment service integrated with the **Stripe API** and an email service using **SendGrid**, we demonstrated how microservices can communicate with external services to enhance the functionality of an application. These integrations allow microservices to delegate specific tasks (such as payments or emails) to specialized, third-party services, enabling the system to scale more efficiently and focus on its core functionalities.

As the use of third-party APIs continues to grow, microservices must be designed with flexibility, scalability, and resilience in mind to ensure smooth communication with external services. By implementing robust error handling, authentication, and rate limiting, you can build reliable systems that integrate with the broader ecosystem of external APIs.

CHAPTER 13: EVENT-DRIVEN ARCHITECTURE IN MICROSERVICES

As microservices architectures evolve, they become more complex, and ensuring that different services can communicate efficiently and asynchronously becomes essential. One of the most powerful patterns that can handle this complexity is **event-driven architecture (EDA)**. In an event-driven system, components of the system communicate with each other by producing and consuming events, which represent state changes or triggers for other services. This enables loose coupling between microservices, improves scalability, and provides better resilience for the system.

In this chapter, we will explore the **key concepts** of event-driven architecture, including **event sourcing**, **CQRS** (Command Query Responsibility Segregation), and how event-driven systems function. We will use **LinkedIn** as a real-world example of how event-driven architectures are used in large-scale, distributed systems. Additionally, we will walk through a tutorial on **setting up an event-driven service using Kafka** and provide a project where we implement an event-driven service to **track user activity** and trigger **notifications**.

Key Concepts

1. Event-Driven Architecture (EDA)

Event-driven architecture is a software architecture pattern where components of the system communicate by producing and consuming events. An event is a message that signifies a change in state or an occurrence in the system. These events are processed asynchronously, making EDA an ideal solution for decoupled, distributed systems where different microservices need to react to certain changes or triggers.

Characteristics of Event-Driven Architecture:

- **Loose Coupling:** Components do not directly communicate with one another. Instead, they publish events, and other components consume them.

- **Asynchronous Communication:** Events are processed asynchronously, meaning the producer does not wait for the consumer to process the event.

- **Scalability:** Event-driven systems are highly scalable as services can scale independently depending on their consumption of events.

- **Resilience and Fault Tolerance:** If a service goes down, it does not directly affect the rest of the system, as events can be queued or stored until the service recovers.

Event-driven architectures often use a **message broker** (such as **Apache Kafka**, **RabbitMQ**, or **Amazon SQS**) to manage the delivery of events from producers to consumers.

2. Event Sourcing

Event sourcing is an architectural pattern where changes to the system's state are stored as a sequence of **events** rather than updating the state directly in a database. The state of the system can then be reconstructed by replaying these events in the order in which they occurred.

Advantages of Event Sourcing:

- **Auditability:** Since all changes to the system are stored as events, you have a complete audit trail of all actions and state transitions.

- **Reconstruction of State:** The current state of the system can be reconstructed by replaying events, which is particularly useful in debugging or recovering from failures.

- **Flexibility:** You can replay events or project different views of the system's state for various use cases (e.g., reporting, analytics).

Event Sourcing vs. Traditional Databases:

In traditional systems, state changes are written directly to the database as updates to records. In event sourcing, each change in state is represented as an immutable event that is appended to an event store. This allows for a more granular and auditable view of changes over time.

3. CQRS (Command Query Responsibility Segregation)

CQRS is a pattern where the system is split into two parts:

- **Command Side:** This side handles operations that modify the state of the system (e.g., creating, updating, or deleting data). Commands are usually processed asynchronously, and they often interact with the event store in event-driven systems.

- **Query Side:** This side handles read operations and does not modify the state. It is optimized for querying data and can be implemented using denormalized views or read-optimized data stores.

How CQRS Fits with Event-Driven Systems:

In an event-driven architecture, the **command side** generates events, which can then be processed by consumers that update the read models (query side). This separation allows for optimization and scaling of each side independently. The **command side** is often more complex and optimized for write-heavy workloads, while the **query side** is optimized for read-heavy operations.

4. Event-Driven Systems: Benefits and Challenges

Benefits of Event-Driven Systems:

- **Loose Coupling:** Services are decoupled, as they communicate via events instead of direct calls. This makes it easier to develop, maintain, and scale individual services.

- **Asynchronous Processing:** The system can handle high volumes of requests more efficiently by processing events asynchronously, enabling non-blocking operations.

- **Scalability and Flexibility:** Event-driven systems can scale more easily because individual components can be scaled independently based on demand.

- **Real-Time Processing:** Event-driven systems are excellent for use cases that require real-time processing or immediate reaction to changes in state (e.g., fraud detection, notifications, data analytics).

Challenges of Event-Driven Systems:

- **Eventual Consistency:** Since events are processed asynchronously, systems must be designed to handle eventual consistency, where the state across microservices may not always be synchronized in real-time.

- **Complexity in Debugging:** Debugging can be more difficult because the system state is based on the sequence of events rather than the current state in a database.

- **Event Duplication and Ordering:** Handling duplicate events and ensuring they are processed in the correct order is essential for maintaining consistency in the system.

Real-World Example: How LinkedIn Handles Event-Driven Architectures for Scalable Systems

LinkedIn, one of the largest social networking platforms, uses an event-driven architecture to scale its systems effectively. The platform processes billions of interactions daily, including **messages, connections, job updates**, and **notifications**. To handle this, LinkedIn employs event-driven architecture patterns at multiple levels of their infrastructure.

1. Event-Driven Approach for Notifications

LinkedIn uses an event-driven approach to manage **notifications**. When a user interacts with the platform (e.g., sending a message, liking a post, or connecting with someone), the system generates an event. This event is consumed by different services that handle specific tasks, such as sending an email, push notification, or updating the activity feed.

- **Producers:** When an action occurs (like a new message or connection request), an event is produced by the relevant service (e.g., the **Messaging Service** or **Connections Service**).

- **Consumers:** Other services (e.g., **Notification Service**, **Feed Service**) consume the event to trigger appropriate actions, like sending notifications or updating the feed.

2. Event Sourcing in LinkedIn's Architecture

LinkedIn also uses **event sourcing** to track changes to user activity, such as profile updates, post engagements, or job changes. Events are stored in an event store, and the current state of a user's profile or feed can be reconstructed by replaying the relevant events.

For example, when a user changes their profile, the event representing the change is stored and can be replayed to rebuild the profile's state at any point in time. This approach helps LinkedIn ensure that all changes are auditable and consistent across its microservices.

3. CQRS for Handling High Throughput

LinkedIn uses **CQRS** to handle high-throughput systems such as job feeds and notifications. The **command side** handles the creation and update of events (e.g., a user posts a job opening or updates their status), while the **query side** provides read-optimized views, allowing users to quickly search and browse job listings or news feeds.

By separating commands from queries, LinkedIn can scale each part of the system independently and optimize them for different workloads.

Tutorial: Setting Up an Event-Driven Service Using Kafka

Apache Kafka is a distributed event streaming platform used for building real-time data pipelines and streaming applications. It is often used in event-driven architectures for event storage, message queuing, and stream processing.

Step 1: Install Apache Kafka

1. **Install Kafka Locally:** You can install Kafka on your local machine or use a managed Kafka service. To install it locally, follow the instructions from the Apache Kafka website.

2. **Start Zookeeper and Kafka:** Kafka depends on Zookeeper, so you must first start Zookeeper and then Kafka:

bash

bin/zookeeper-server-start.sh config/zookeeper.properties

bin/kafka-server-start.sh config/server.properties

Step 2: Create Kafka Topics

Topics are logical channels to which producers send events and consumers read from. For this tutorial, we will create two topics: user-activity and notification-events.

bash

```
bin/kafka-topics.sh --create --topic user-activity --bootstrap-
server localhost:9092 --partitions 1 --replication-factor 1
```

```
bin/kafka-topics.sh --create --topic notification-events --
bootstrap-server    localhost:9092    --partitions    1    --
replication-factor 1
```

Step 3: Producer Service

The producer will send events to Kafka when a user performs an activity (e.g., logging in or updating their profile).

1. **Add Kafka Dependencies:** In your **Spring Boot** project, add the following dependencies to the pom.xml file:

xml

```xml
<dependency>
    <groupId>org.springframework.kafka</groupId>
```

```
    <artifactId>spring-kafka</artifactId>
</dependency>
```

2. Producer Service:

java

```java
@Service
public class UserActivityProducer {

    private final KafkaTemplate<String, String>
kafkaTemplate;

    @Value("${kafka.topic.user-activity}")
    private String topic;

    public UserActivityProducer(KafkaTemplate<String,
String> kafkaTemplate) {
        this.kafkaTemplate = kafkaTemplate;
    }

    public void sendUserActivity(String userId, String activity)
{
```

```java
        String event = String.format("User: %s, Activity: %s",
userId, activity);

        kafkaTemplate.send(topic, userId, event);

    }

}
```

In this producer, the sendUserActivity() method sends a message to the user-activity Kafka topic.

Step 4: Consumer Service

The consumer listens for events from Kafka and processes them accordingly. In this case, we'll consume the user activity and trigger a notification event.

1. **Consumer Service:**

java

```java
@Service
public class NotificationEventConsumer {

    @KafkaListener(topics = "user-activity", groupId =
"notification-group")
    public void consumeUserActivity(String activityEvent) {
        // Trigger notification
```

```
System.out.println("Received activity event: " +
activityEvent);
    // Add your notification logic here (e.g., send email, push
notification)
  }
}
```

This consumer listens to the user-activity topic and processes the event by triggering a notification.

Step 5: Testing the Event-Driven Service

1. **Run Kafka Producer and Consumer:** Ensure your Kafka broker is running. Then start your application, which will automatically start producing and consuming events.

2. **Send an Event:** Use Postman or curl to send an HTTP request to trigger the producer:

bash

```
curl -X POST http://localhost:8080/activity -d '{"userId":
"123", "activity": "Logged in"}' -H "Content-Type:
application/json"
```

3. **Check the Consumer Logs:** The consumer service should log the received activity event, and you can further expand this to trigger actual notifications.

Project: Implement an Event-Driven Service to Track User Activity and Trigger Notifications

In this project, we will build a complete event-driven system that tracks user activity and sends notifications based on that activity. This system will include:

1. **User Activity Producer:** The microservice that generates user activity events.

2. **Notification Consumer:** The microservice that listens for user activity events and triggers notifications.

3. **Kafka Broker:** Used to transmit events between the producer and consumer.

Step 1: Setting Up Kafka

Follow the instructions in the tutorial to install **Kafka** locally or use a cloud-based Kafka service like **Confluent Cloud**.

Step 2: Implementing the Producer and Consumer Services

Build the producer and consumer services as demonstrated above, ensuring they can produce and consume events via **Kafka**.

Step 3: Testing and Scaling the System

To test the system:

1. Trigger user activity events via the producer (e.g., user login, purchase).

2. Ensure that notifications are generated based on these activities.

3. Use **Kafka**'s partitioning and scaling features to test how the system performs under load.

By scaling the consumer service, you can ensure that the system can handle high throughput of events, such as a surge in user activity.

Conclusion

In this chapter, we explored the power of **event-driven architecture** for microservices, covering concepts like

event sourcing, CQRS, and **event-driven systems**. We demonstrated how **LinkedIn** uses event-driven patterns for scalable systems and provided a detailed tutorial on setting up an event-driven service using **Kafka**. The project showed how to integrate user activity tracking and notification triggering using Kafka as the messaging platform.

Event-driven architectures are essential for building scalable, resilient, and flexible systems, especially as microservices architectures grow in complexity. By adopting event-driven patterns, organizations can decouple services, scale them independently, and build robust systems that respond to real-time events effectively.

CHAPTER 14: ADVANCED MICROSERVICES SECURITY AND COMPLIANCE

As microservices architectures become the standard for large-scale applications, ensuring the security and compliance of these systems has never been more critical. Microservices architectures introduce a range of security challenges, from protecting sensitive data to managing the authentication and authorization of thousands of services and users. With multiple services interacting over a network, each component must be secured, and communication must be authenticated and encrypted. Additionally, as privacy laws such as the **General Data Protection Regulation (GDPR)** come into play, ensuring compliance becomes an increasingly important aspect of managing microservices systems.

In this chapter, we will cover the **key concepts** of security in large-scale microservices, including best practices for securing services, managing compliance, and ensuring privacy. We will dive into how organizations like **Netflix** manage security across their distributed systems, followed by a **tutorial** on implementing **Role-Based Access Control (RBAC)** in a microservices setup. Lastly, we will walk through a **project** on securing a microservices application with **OAuth2** and implementing **compliance checks** to meet GDPR requirements.

Key Concepts

1. Security Challenges in Microservices

Microservices architectures pose unique security challenges due to their distributed nature, decentralized management, and complex service-to-service communication. Below are some of the key security challenges in microservices:

1.1 Authentication and Authorization

Microservices typically rely on multiple services to handle requests, which can make it difficult to authenticate and authorize users. Each microservice might need to validate the identity of the user or the service calling it. There are two core challenges:

- **Service-to-Service Authentication:** Ensuring that communication between microservices is authenticated and authorized. One compromised service can potentially affect the entire system.

- **User Authentication:** Users must be authenticated once and their identity must be passed securely between services (typically using **JWT (JSON Web Tokens) or OAuth2 tokens**).

1.2 Data Protection and Encryption

Since data is passed across multiple microservices and databases, it's critical to ensure that it is encrypted both in transit and at rest. Sensitive data such as personal information, payment details, or confidential business data should be protected using encryption methods such as **SSL/TLS** for in-transit data and encryption standards like **AES-256** for stored data.

1.3 API Security

Microservices communicate with each other through APIs, which are often public-facing. Securing these APIs is crucial. Some of the security practices include:

- **Rate Limiting:** Preventing abuse by limiting the number of requests to a service within a given time frame.

- **Input Validation:** Ensuring that inputs to the API are sanitized to avoid attacks such as SQL injection or cross-site scripting (XSS).

- **Access Control:** Limiting access to APIs to only authorized users or services.

1.4 Distributed Denial of Service (DDoS) Protection

Microservices, being distributed systems, are more exposed to **DDoS** attacks due to the numerous entry points across services. Security tools and rate limiting should be employed to mitigate these threats and ensure that the system remains available during peak loads or malicious attempts to overload the system.

1.5 Security at Scale

The sheer number of services in a large microservices architecture can make security difficult to maintain. Each service may have its own set of security requirements, such as encryption, authentication, and logging. Keeping track of all security configurations across services requires effective management tools and automation.

2. Best Practices for Securing Microservices

To address the challenges outlined above, microservices should be designed with security as a foundational component. Below are some best practices to ensure the security of large-scale microservices architectures:

2.1 Use API Gateways for Centralized Security Management

An **API gateway** can act as a central point of control for authentication, authorization, rate limiting, and logging. By centralizing these concerns, you reduce the complexity of implementing them in each individual service.

2.2 Implement Role-Based Access Control (RBAC)

RBAC allows you to define what actions users and services are allowed to perform. By controlling access based on the roles assigned to users or services, you can limit access to sensitive data or critical functionalities.

2.3 Secure Communication with TLS/SSL

Using **SSL/TLS** to secure communication between microservices ensures that data is encrypted in transit. All communication, whether between internal services or with external clients, should use secure channels to prevent interception and tampering.

2.4 Use OAuth2 for Secure and Scalable Authentication

OAuth2 provides a robust framework for securing user and service authentication, especially in systems with many independent services. Using **JWT tokens** to authenticate API calls provides stateless, scalable authentication across services.

2.5 Data Privacy and GDPR Compliance

For services that process user data, ensuring compliance with regulations like the **General Data Protection Regulation (GDPR)** is critical. This involves implementing proper consent mechanisms, allowing users to access, modify, or delete their data, and ensuring data is protected according to regulatory standards.

2.6 Implement Centralized Logging and Monitoring

Logging and monitoring across microservices allow for real-time threat detection. Tools like **ELK stack** (Elasticsearch, Logstash, and Kibana), **Prometheus**, and **Grafana** can be used to monitor the health of microservices, detect anomalies, and trace security incidents across the system.

2.7 Use Zero Trust Architecture

In a **Zero Trust** model, no entity, whether inside or outside the network, is trusted by default. Every request is treated as potentially malicious and must be authenticated, authorized, and encrypted before it can access resources. This is crucial in distributed systems like microservices, where the attack surface is vast.

Real-World Example: How Netflix Ensures Security for Its Distributed Systems

Netflix, a leader in the streaming industry, operates one of the most complex microservices architectures in the world. With millions of users accessing their platform across different regions and devices, ensuring the security of their microservices is a top priority. Here's how Netflix handles security for its distributed systems:

1. Authentication and Authorization with OAuth2

Netflix uses **OAuth2** for authentication and authorization, particularly for user and service access. For service-to-service communication, Netflix utilizes **JWT tokens**, which allow each service to authenticate its requests without needing to store session information. This enables **stateless authentication**, a key requirement for scalable microservices systems.

2. Use of API Gateways for Security

Netflix uses an API gateway that acts as the first line of defense for incoming requests. The gateway handles:

- **Authentication:** Ensuring that users are authenticated before they can interact with the microservices.

- **Rate Limiting:** Protecting services from DDoS attacks by limiting the number of requests.

- **Access Control:** Ensuring that only authorized users can access specific services.

3. Service Mesh and Encryption

Netflix uses a **service mesh** (such as **Envoy** or **Istio**) for service-to-service communication. The service mesh provides features such as **traffic encryption** and **mutual TLS (mTLS)** to ensure that all communication between services is secure.

4. Event-Driven Architecture for Auditing and Monitoring

Netflix uses an event-driven approach to manage logs and monitor user activity. Every action on the platform, such as logging in, viewing content, or interacting with the UI, triggers an event that is processed asynchronously. These events are stored in a **distributed log** and used to audit and track security incidents.

5. Continuous Compliance with GDPR

Netflix operates across different jurisdictions, including the EU, where GDPR applies. To ensure compliance, Netflix implements the following practices:

- **Data Minimization:** Collecting only the necessary data for delivering services.

- **User Rights:** Allowing users to view, modify, and delete their personal data.

- **Consent Management:** Ensuring that users are aware of and consent to how their data will be used.

By following these principles, Netflix ensures that its distributed systems are both secure and compliant with the latest regulations.

Tutorial: Implementing Role-Based Access Control (RBAC) in a Microservices Setup

In this tutorial, we will demonstrate how to implement **Role-Based Access Control (RBAC)** in a microservices environment. RBAC is a model for restricting access to resources based on the roles of individual users within an organization.

Step 1: Define Roles and Permissions

Before implementing RBAC, we need to define the roles and permissions for our application. Let's assume our application has the following roles:

- **Admin:** Full access to all resources.

- **User:** Limited access to their personal data and activity.

- **Guest:** Only read access to publicly available data.

Each role will have associated permissions, such as creating, updating, or deleting data.

Step 2: Implementing Authentication and Authorization

For this tutorial, we will use **Spring Security** and **JWT tokens** to authenticate and authorize users in a Spring Boot-based microservices application.

1. **Add Spring Security and JWT Dependencies:**

xml

```xml
<dependency>
    <groupId>org.springframework.boot</groupId>
    <artifactId>spring-boot-starter-security</artifactId>
```

```
</dependency>
<dependency>
    <groupId>io.jsonwebtoken</groupId>
    <artifactId>jjwt</artifactId>
</dependency>
```

2. Create the Role and User Models:

java

```java
@Entity
public class User {

    @Id
    @GeneratedValue(strategy = GenerationType.IDENTITY)
    private Long id;
    private String username;
    private String password;
    @ManyToMany(fetch = FetchType.EAGER)
    private Set<Role> roles;

    // Getters and setters omitted for brevity
}
```

```java
@Entity
public class Role {

    @Id
    @GeneratedValue(strategy = GenerationType.IDENTITY)
    private Long id;
    private String name;

    // Getters and setters omitted for brevity
}
```

3. **Configure Spring Security:**

In your SecurityConfig class, define access rules for different roles.

java

```java
@Configuration
@EnableWebSecurity
public class SecurityConfig extends
WebSecurityConfigurerAdapter {

    @Override
```

```
protected void configure(HttpSecurity http) throws
Exception {
    http
        .authorizeRequests()
        .antMatchers("/admin/**").hasRole("ADMIN")
        .antMatchers("/user/**").hasAnyRole("USER",
"ADMIN")
        .antMatchers("/guest/**").permitAll()
        .and()
        .formLogin();
    }
}
```

This configuration ensures that only users with the ADMIN role can access /admin/**, and only USER and ADMIN roles can access /user/**.

Step 3: Generating and Validating JWT Tokens

JWT tokens are used to represent the identity and roles of users. When a user logs in, a token is generated with their role information, which can then be used to authenticate requests.

1. Create a JWT Utility Class:

java

```java
public class JwtUtil {

    private String secretKey = "your-secret-key";

    public String generateToken(User user) {
        return Jwts.builder()
                .setSubject(user.getUsername())
                .claim("roles",
user.getRoles().stream().map(Role::getName).collect(Collectors.toList()))
                .signWith(SignatureAlgorithm.HS256, secretKey)
                .compact();
    }

    public Claims extractClaims(String token) {
        return Jwts.parser()
                .setSigningKey(secretKey)
                .parseClaimsJws(token)
                .getBody();
```

```
    }

    public String extractUsername(String token) {
        return extractClaims(token).getSubject();
    }

    public List<String> extractRoles(String token) {
        return (List<String>) extractClaims(token).get("roles");
    }

    public boolean isTokenExpired(String token) {
        return extractClaims(token).getExpiration().before(new
Date());
    }

    public boolean validateToken(String token, UserDetails
userDetails) {
        return
(userDetails.getUsername().equals(extractUsername(token))
&& !isTokenExpired(token));
    }
}
```

2. JWT Filter for Role-Based Access:

java

```java
public class JwtAuthenticationFilter extends
OncePerRequestFilter {

    private JwtUtil jwtUtil;

    public JwtAuthenticationFilter(JwtUtil jwtUtil) {
        this.jwtUtil = jwtUtil;
    }

    @Override
    protected void doFilterInternal(HttpServletRequest request,
HttpServletResponse response, FilterChain chain)
            throws ServletException, IOException {
        String token = request.getHeader("Authorization");

        if (token != null && token.startsWith("Bearer ")) {
            token = token.substring(7);
            String username = jwtUtil.extractUsername(token);
            List<String> roles = jwtUtil.extractRoles(token);
```

```
        // Implement authentication logic

    }


    chain.doFilter(request, response);

  }

}
```

Step 4: Testing and Verifying RBAC

After setting up the JWT-based authentication and RBAC, test the system by attempting to access endpoints with different roles. Use tools like **Postman** or **cURL** to make requests with various user roles and ensure that the access control works as expected.

Project: Secure Your Application with OAuth2 and Implement Compliance Checks

In this project, we will secure a microservices application using **OAuth2** and implement **compliance checks** for **GDPR**.

Step 1: Set Up OAuth2 Authentication

OAuth2 allows you to delegate authentication and authorization to a trusted third-party service, such as **Google, GitHub,** or an **internal OAuth server**.

1. **Add OAuth2 Dependencies:**

xml

```
<dependency>
    <groupId>org.springframework.boot</groupId>
    <artifactId>spring-boot-starter-oauth2-client</artifactId>
</dependency>
```

2. **Configure OAuth2 Login:**

In the application.yml or application.properties, configure the OAuth2 client:

yaml

```
spring:
  security:
    oauth2:
      client:
        registration:
          google:
```

```
client-id: your-client-id

client-secret: your-client-secret

scope: profile, email

redirect-uri:
```
"{baseUrl}/login/oauth2/code/{registrationId}"

3. Secure the Microservices Using OAuth2:

java

```java
@EnableOAuth2Sso
@Configuration
public class OAuth2SecurityConfig extends
WebSecurityConfigurerAdapter {

    @Override
    protected void configure(HttpSecurity http) throws
Exception {
        http
            .authorizeRequests()
            .antMatchers("/private/**").authenticated()
            .anyRequest().permitAll()
            .and()
            .oauth2Login();
```

```
    }
}
```

Step 2: Implement GDPR Compliance

To ensure **GDPR compliance**, implement features like:

- **Data Subject Access Requests (DSAR):** Allow users to request their personal data.

- **Data Deletion:** Allow users to delete their personal data.

- **Data Minimization:** Ensure that only the necessary data is collected and stored.

1. **Data Deletion Endpoint:**

java

```java
@RestController
public class DataComplianceController {

    @DeleteMapping("/user/data")
    public ResponseEntity<String>
deleteUserData(@RequestParam Long userId) {
        // Implement logic to delete personal data from databases
```

```java
    return ResponseEntity.ok("User data deleted
successfully.");
  }
}
```

2. **Data Access Requests (DSAR):**

```java
java

@RestController
public class DataRequestController {

  @GetMapping("/user/data")
  public ResponseEntity<String>
getUserData(@RequestParam Long userId) {
    // Implement logic to retrieve personal data
    return ResponseEntity.ok("User data: ...");
  }
}
```

By implementing these features, your application will meet essential GDPR requirements.

Conclusion

In this chapter, we explored advanced security practices for large-scale microservices, including **authentication**, **authorization**, and **compliance with GDPR**. We discussed how microservices systems need to be secured at every layer, from ensuring service-to-service communication is secure to protecting user data and implementing role-based access control.

We also walked through real-world examples of how **Netflix** secures its distributed systems and provided a tutorial on implementing **RBAC** using **JWT** tokens. Finally, we demonstrated how to secure a microservices application with **OAuth2** and implement compliance checks to ensure **GDPR** compliance.

By following these best practices, microservices systems can be secured against a range of threats, ensuring privacy, compliance, and resilience in distributed environments.

CHAPTER 15: FUTURE TRENDS AND EMERGING TECHNOLOGIES IN MICROSERVICES

The world of microservices is continuously evolving, with new technologies and paradigms reshaping how distributed systems are built, deployed, and scaled. As enterprises increasingly adopt microservices to break down monolithic applications, the next wave of innovation is emerging. This chapter explores the **future trends** and **emerging technologies** in the microservices space, including **serverless architecture**, **AI/ML integrations**, and **edge computing**. We will also dive into how these technologies are transforming event-driven applications, and how microservices can integrate with these advancements to become more efficient and scalable.

We'll explore the following key concepts:

- **Serverless Architecture**

- **AI/ML Integrations in Microservices**

- **Edge Computing in Microservices**

- **Real-World Examples** of how companies are adopting these technologies

- **A hands-on tutorial** for setting up a simple **serverless service with AWS Lambda**

- A **project** that explores how **serverless architecture** can complement your existing microservices design.

Key Concepts

1. Serverless Architecture

Serverless architecture is a cloud computing model where cloud providers automatically manage the infrastructure for applications. In the context of microservices, serverless platforms allow developers to build and deploy applications without worrying about managing servers. The serverless model is ideal for **event-driven** applications, where functions are triggered by specific events or requests.

How Serverless Works

- **Event-Driven:** Serverless functions are triggered by events such as HTTP requests, file uploads, or changes to a database.

- **No Server Management:** Serverless abstracts away the management of physical or virtual servers. The cloud provider automatically provisions, scales, and manages the resources needed to run the application.

- **Pay-as-You-Go Model:** Users are billed based on the actual execution time of their functions, which makes serverless highly cost-effective, particularly for sporadic or low-traffic services.

Benefits of Serverless in Microservices

- **Cost Efficiency:** Serverless eliminates the need for provisioning idle resources. You only pay for actual usage, and resources are automatically scaled up or down based on demand.

- **Scalability:** Serverless platforms like **AWS Lambda** or **Google Cloud Functions** automatically scale to handle varying loads. No need for manual scaling or load balancing.

- **Focus on Code:** Developers can focus on writing functions or logic rather than managing infrastructure.

- **Faster Time to Market:** With serverless, applications can be developed and deployed faster because the overhead of managing servers is eliminated.

Challenges of Serverless

- **Cold Starts:** Serverless functions can experience **cold start** latency when they haven't been executed recently. This occurs because the cloud provider must spin up new instances of the function.

- **State Management:** Since serverless functions are stateless by nature, managing state across multiple function calls can be challenging.

- **Vendor Lock-In:** Using a specific serverless provider like AWS Lambda or Google Cloud Functions may lead to vendor lock-in, making it difficult to move between providers.

---

2. AI/ML Integrations in Microservices

Artificial Intelligence (AI) and Machine Learning (ML) are rapidly transforming the landscape of software development, and integrating AI/ML capabilities into microservices is becoming increasingly important. AI/ML allows microservices to become smarter by analyzing data, making predictions, automating tasks, and improving decision-making processes.

Use Cases for AI/ML in Microservices

- **Personalization:** AI-driven microservices can be used to personalize user experiences, such as recommending products or content based on user behavior.

- **Data Analytics:** Microservices can process large volumes of data and provide insights into patterns or trends that can drive business decisions.

- **Automation:** AI-powered microservices can automate tasks that previously required human intervention, such as detecting fraud or managing inventory.

- **Predictive Modeling:** Machine learning models can be integrated into microservices to predict future trends, like sales forecasts or customer churn rates.

AI/ML Technologies for Microservices

- **TensorFlow**, **PyTorch**, and **Scikit-Learn** are commonly used machine learning frameworks that can be deployed as microservices for real-time predictions.

- **AI/ML APIs**: Platforms like **Google AI**, **AWS SageMaker**, and **Azure ML** provide managed services for integrating machine learning models into microservices.

Challenges of AI/ML in Microservices

- **Complexity:** Integrating AI/ML models into microservices can be complex, especially when dealing with large datasets or real-time processing.

- **Model Updates:** AI/ML models need to be continuously updated and retrained to ensure accuracy. Managing these updates and deploying them without downtime can be challenging.

- **Performance Overheads:** Running AI/ML models in microservices may introduce latency, especially for complex models or large datasets.

---

3. Edge Computing in Microservices

Edge computing refers to the practice of processing data closer to the source of data generation, at the "edge" of the network, rather than in centralized cloud servers. In microservices, edge computing allows for **distributed**

computing where microservices are deployed closer to users or devices, thus reducing latency and improving performance.

How Edge Computing Works

- **Data Processing at the Edge:** Data is processed locally on edge devices (e.g., sensors, IoT devices) or local servers, with minimal reliance on the cloud.

- **Decentralized Architecture:** Edge computing enables a decentralized approach to processing data, making it ideal for real-time applications like autonomous vehicles, smart cities, and industrial IoT.

Benefits of Edge Computing in Microservices

- **Low Latency:** By processing data closer to the source, edge computing reduces the latency caused by transmitting data to centralized servers.

- **Bandwidth Efficiency:** Only necessary data is sent to the cloud, reducing the bandwidth and cost associated with transmitting large volumes of data.

- **Improved Resilience:** Edge computing allows for continued operation even if connectivity to the central server is lost, as data can be processed and acted upon locally.

Challenges of Edge Computing

- **Security:** Edge devices are more vulnerable to physical attacks, and securing the data transfer between the edge and the cloud is crucial.

- **Management:** Managing a large number of distributed edge devices can be complex, requiring efficient monitoring, updates, and fault detection.

- **Scalability:** Edge computing can be difficult to scale due to the distributed nature of the system.

Real-World Example: How Companies Are Moving Towards Serverless for Event-Driven Applications

Many companies are adopting serverless architectures, especially for event-driven applications. Here are two notable examples:

1. Airbnb's Event-Driven Architecture with Serverless

Airbnb uses serverless architecture to handle various event-driven tasks such as notifications, image processing, and log analysis. By using **AWS Lambda**, Airbnb eliminates the need to provision servers for these tasks, making it easier to scale and improve resource utilization.

Airbnb's system triggers Lambda functions based on events such as a new booking, a payment completion, or a user interaction. These functions perform tasks like sending confirmation emails or processing images for listings. The serverless model allows Airbnb to respond quickly to these events without worrying about managing infrastructure.

2. Uber's Use of Serverless for Data Processing

Uber also leverages serverless technologies for managing their **data pipelines**. They use **AWS Lambda** to process real-time data streams such as ride requests, payments, and driver availability. By using serverless computing, Uber can handle vast amounts of event-driven data with minimal delay, scaling the processing capacity dynamically based on the volume of incoming data.

Uber also uses **event-driven** architectures for real-time communication between services, including notifications for users and drivers, as well as payment processing events.

Tutorial: Setting Up a Simple Serverless Service with AWS Lambda

In this tutorial, we will set up a **serverless service** using **AWS Lambda** to handle an event-driven task. We'll create a simple service that listens to an event (e.g., a new user registration) and triggers a Lambda function to process it, such as sending a welcome email.

Step 1: Set Up an AWS Account

If you don't already have an AWS account, go to AWS and sign up for a free account. AWS offers a free tier for Lambda, API Gateway, and other services, so you can get started without incurring charges.

Step 2: Create a Lambda Function

1. **Log in to AWS Console:** Navigate to the AWS Management Console and search for **Lambda**.

2. **Create a New Lambda Function:** Click on **Create function** and select the **Author from scratch** option.

   o **Function name:** UserRegistrationHandler

- Runtime: Choose **Node.js** (or your preferred language).

- Role: Choose **Create a new role with basic Lambda permissions**.

3. **Write the Lambda Function Code:** The function will be triggered when a new user registers. In this example, we will simulate sending a welcome email.

javascript

```javascript
const AWS = require('aws-sdk');
const SES = new AWS.SES({ region: 'us-east-1' });

exports.handler = async (event) => {
  const emailParams = {
    Destination: {
      ToAddresses: [event.userEmail],
    },
    Message: {
      Body: {
        Text: {
          Data: 'Welcome to our service!',
        },
      },
```

```
      Subject: {
          Data: 'Welcome to our platform!',
      },
    },
    Source: 'no-reply@yourdomain.com',
  };


  try {
    await SES.sendEmail(emailParams).promise();
    console.log('Welcome email sent successfully.');
  } catch (err) {
    console.error('Error sending email:', err);
    throw new Error('Email sending failed');
  }


  return {
    statusCode: 200,
    body: JSON.stringify('Email sent successfully!'),
  };
};
```

This function uses **AWS SES (Simple Email Service)** to send a welcome email to the new user's email address.

4. **Deploy the Lambda Function:** Click **Deploy** to deploy your Lambda function.

Step 3: Set Up an API Gateway

1. **Create a New API Gateway:** Go to the **API Gateway** service in AWS and create a new REST API.

2. **Create a Resource:** Add a new resource to the API, such as /user-registration.

3. **Create a POST Method:** Under the /user-registration resource, create a new **POST** method and link it to the Lambda function you created earlier.

4. **Deploy the API:** Deploy the API to a new stage (e.g., dev).

Step 4: Test the Serverless Service

You can now test the serverless service using **Postman** or **cURL**. Send a POST request to the API Gateway URL with the new user's information:

bash

POST https://your-api-id.execute-api.us-east-1.amazonaws.com/dev/user-registration

Content-Type: application/json

```
{

  "userEmail": "newuser@example.com"

}
```

The Lambda function will be triggered, sending a welcome email to the user's email address.

Project: Explore How Serverless Architecture Can Complement Your Existing Microservices Design

Serverless architecture can complement existing microservices in several ways:

1. Offload Asynchronous Tasks to Serverless

For tasks that are event-driven and don't need to be processed by your core microservices, you can use serverless functions to handle them. For example:

- **Image processing** (e.g., resizing user-uploaded images)

- **Notification services** (e.g., sending email, SMS, or push notifications)

2. API Gateway Integration

Use **API Gateway** to expose REST APIs for your existing microservices and combine them with serverless functions for handling specific tasks, such as payments, user authentication, or logging.

3. Event-Driven Microservices

Combine serverless with **event-driven architectures** to trigger Lambda functions based on events from microservices. For example, when a new order is placed, a Lambda function could be triggered to update a separate service or notify users.

4. Cost Efficiency

In microservices architectures, serverless can help optimize costs by offloading unpredictable workloads or rarely used services. For instance, instead of running a dedicated service for generating reports every day, you could use serverless to generate reports on-demand.

Conclusion

In this chapter, we explored several **emerging technologies** in microservices architectures, including **serverless, AI/ML integrations**, and **edge computing**. We saw how serverless architecture can simplify the management and scalability of microservices by allowing developers to focus on writing business logic while the infrastructure is automatically managed.

We also explored **real-world examples** such as how companies like **Airbnb** and **Uber** leverage serverless for event-driven applications, and how **Netflix** implements AI/ML and event-driven systems in their architecture. Through the hands-on tutorial, we set up a simple serverless service with **AWS Lambda**, and in the project, we explored how **serverless architecture** can complement existing microservices to enhance efficiency and scalability.

As microservices continue to evolve, adopting emerging technologies like **serverless, AI/ML**, and **edge computing** will empower organizations to build more efficient, flexible, and scalable applications. These advancements will play a crucial role in shaping the future of microservices.

CONCLUSION: THE JOURNEY AHEAD

As you finish this guide on microservices, it's important to remember that this journey is far from over. What you've learned so far is just the beginning of what will likely be an ongoing exploration into the complexities and power of microservices architectures. In the rapidly evolving world of software development, understanding microservices is not just about knowing how to implement them but also about adapting to new challenges and opportunities as they arise. As we move forward, there are countless possibilities and areas for growth, and I encourage you to continue pushing the boundaries of your knowledge and expertise.

Final Thoughts

Throughout this book, we've covered foundational concepts and advanced techniques for building, deploying, and managing microservices. These concepts, from **service discovery** to **serverless architectures** and **event-driven systems**, lay the groundwork for creating scalable, maintainable, and resilient systems. However, the world of microservices is vast, and there is always more to learn.

As you work on your own projects, whether you're building a small application or scaling a large enterprise system, keep experimenting and learning. The microservices landscape is not static — it is constantly evolving with new tools, frameworks, and patterns that are designed to solve modern challenges in distributed systems. Embrace the opportunity to learn from both your successes and your failures. Each challenge you face is an opportunity to grow and understand more deeply the intricacies of building distributed systems.

Here are a few ways you can continue exploring and applying what you've learned:

1. **Experiment with New Technologies**: The landscape of microservices is vast, and there is always something new to learn. Whether it's a new service mesh like **Istio**, a different event-driven framework, or the latest advancements in container orchestration (e.g., Kubernetes updates), there are plenty of technologies worth exploring.

2. **Contribute to Open-Source Projects**: Open-source microservices projects are a fantastic way to apply what you've learned in a real-world setting. Not only do you get hands-on experience, but you also benefit from the feedback and collaboration of others in the community.

3. **Stay Current with Industry Trends**: Follow blogs, attend webinars, and participate in conferences and meetups focused on microservices and distributed systems. The field is evolving rapidly, and staying up to date with the latest trends will give you a competitive edge.

4. **Refactor Legacy Systems**: If you're working in an environment with monolithic applications, consider applying the microservices patterns you've learned to refactor and break down those monolithic systems. The transition from monoliths to microservices can be a gradual and rewarding journey that forces you to adopt new technologies and patterns.

5. **Focus on Systematic Learning**: Microservices are complex, and deepening your knowledge in specific areas — such as security, scalability, or performance optimization — will help you become an expert in the field. Take courses, read research papers, and engage in hands-on learning to expand your skill set.

Real-World Example

Microservices offer significant benefits in terms of scalability, flexibility, and resilience. However, companies face a range of challenges when scaling microservices architectures, especially as they expand their system, add new services, or encounter increased traffic.

One of the key challenges in scaling microservices is **managing a large number of services**. As the number of services grows, so do the complexities in service coordination, monitoring, deployment, and management. Let's dive into some of the most prominent challenges companies face:

1. Managing Service Sprawl

As organizations adopt microservices, they often start with a small number of services. However, as development progresses and the business grows, the number of services tends to increase. **Service sprawl** occurs when the system has many small services, each responsible for a single business function. This brings several challenges:

- **Versioning**: With so many services, maintaining versioning and compatibility between them becomes increasingly difficult. Even small changes to one service can ripple through the system, requiring updates across many services.

- **Service Discovery**: As the number of services increases, so does the complexity of ensuring that each service can discover and communicate with the others. Solutions like **Kubernetes** and **service meshes** (e.g., **Istio**) can help with service discovery, but scaling them introduces new layers of complexity.

- **Dependency Management:** Managing the dependencies between services can become a nightmare. Services may depend on multiple other services, making it challenging to track changes and ensure that everything works together without breaking the system.

2. Observability and Monitoring

With a large number of microservices in production, **observability** becomes one of the most pressing concerns. Unlike monolithic systems, where monitoring may be as simple as checking a single log file, microservices often require sophisticated tools for tracking logs, metrics, traces, and system health.

- **Distributed Tracing:** Tools like **Jaeger, Zipkin,** and **OpenTelemetry** help trace requests across various microservices. However, tracing in a distributed system can become complex when there are many services, each generating logs and events. These logs must be collected, aggregated, and analyzed in real time.

- **Centralized Logging:** Managing logs at scale is another challenge. **ELK Stack (Elasticsearch, Logstash, and Kibana)** and **Fluentd** are often used to collect and aggregate logs from different microservices. But as the number of services grows, ensuring that logs are useful and timely becomes an increasing challenge.

- **Metrics Collection and Alerting**: Microservices often need specialized metrics that can track not just the performance of individual services but also the overall system's health. Solutions like **Prometheus** and **Grafana** are frequently used for this purpose, but their setup and maintenance can become cumbersome when scaling.

3. Ensuring Consistency and Transactional Integrity

One of the hardest problems in microservices is maintaining **data consistency** and ensuring **transactional integrity** across multiple services. Traditional monolithic applications use a single database, which guarantees consistency and integrity through ACID transactions. However, in microservices, each service often manages its own database, leading to potential issues with consistency and transactions across services.

- **Eventual Consistency**: Microservices often rely on **eventual consistency** rather than strong consistency. For example, a payment service might update a user's balance, while an order service might trigger an event that later updates the inventory service. However, this introduces complexity when trying to ensure that the system is consistent across multiple services, especially in the face of failures.

- **Distributed Transactions**: In scenarios requiring atomic transactions across services (e.g., processing payments and updating inventory), it can be difficult to ensure consistency without traditional transactions. Tools like **SAGA pattern** and **two-phase commit** can help, but they introduce additional complexity.

4. Security at Scale

As the number of services increases, so does the number of entry points into the system. Microservices rely heavily on APIs to communicate, making them highly susceptible to security risks such as **data breaches** or **Denial-of-Service (DoS) attacks**.

- **Service-to-Service Authentication**: Ensuring that microservices authenticate and authorize each other properly is crucial. **OAuth2** and **JWT** tokens are often used for this purpose. However, as the number of services grows, managing security tokens and ensuring that services are correctly authenticated becomes more complex.

- **API Security**: With microservices, there are more APIs to secure, and API keys, rate limiting, and input validation must be enforced at scale to avoid attacks like SQL injection, XSS, and DoS.

- **Compliance and Privacy**: Companies operating in regulated industries (e.g., healthcare, finance) face additional challenges ensuring **GDPR** and **HIPAA** compliance across a microservices system. Ensuring that data is protected in accordance with privacy laws is a constant challenge when handling personal information across multiple services.

Actionable Insight

As we've seen, the microservices landscape is complex and continually evolving. The key to mastering microservices is **continuous learning** and **experimentation**. In the fast-paced world of software development, staying updated with new technologies, tools, and architectural patterns is essential to keeping your systems scalable, secure, and resilient.

Here are a few actionable insights to help you stay ahead in the microservices space:

1. Embrace a Culture of Experimentation

Microservices, by their very nature, are experimental. They enable **rapid iteration** and **fast experimentation** due to their modularity and decentralized design. You can try out new technologies, replace components, or experiment with different patterns without disrupting the entire system. For example, you might:

- Test a new database solution (e.g., replacing a traditional relational database with **Cassandra** or **MongoDB**).

- Experiment with a new **service mesh** like **Istio** to handle service-to-service communication.

- Try integrating **AI/ML** models into your microservices to personalize user experiences.

Experimenting with these tools and technologies, while also keeping an eye on their impact on your system's performance, security, and maintainability, will help you evolve your microservices system over time.

2. Participate in Communities and Open Source Projects

The **microservices community** is active and vibrant, with plenty of open-source projects, discussions, and meetups focused on solving real-world problems in microservices architectures. Engage with the community, contribute to open-source projects, and learn from the experiences of others. This will help you gain insights into best practices and avoid common pitfalls that others have already encountered.

- **Contribute to Open Source**: Open-source microservices frameworks such as **Spring Boot**, **Micronaut**, or **Helidon** often rely on contributions from the community. Contributing not only helps you improve your skills but also connects you with like-minded professionals.

- **Attend Conferences and Meetups**: Conferences like **KubeCon**, **Microservices Summit**, and **DevOpsDays** provide excellent opportunities to learn from industry experts, attend workshops, and network with peers in the microservices space.

3. Focus on Practical Applications

As you continue to learn about microservices, it's important to apply theoretical knowledge to practical use cases. The best way to cement your understanding is by building real-world projects. Whether it's designing a system for a small startup or refactoring a legacy monolithic application into microservices, hands-on experience is invaluable.

- **Build Projects**: Start with small projects, such as a simple e-commerce platform, to learn the ins and outs of microservices design and deployment.

- **Refactor Monolithic Applications**: If you're working in a company that relies on a monolithic architecture, consider using microservices to refactor specific components. This gives you practical exposure to the challenges and benefits of transitioning to microservices.

Conclusion

The world of microservices offers enormous potential, but it comes with its own set of challenges. From scaling applications and ensuring security to managing the complexity of multiple services, building a robust and scalable microservices system requires continuous learning, experimentation, and adaptation.

As we've seen, the future of microservices lies in technologies like **serverless, AI/ML integrations**, and **edge computing**, which open new doors for innovation and system efficiency. However, these advancements also introduce new challenges that require developers to stay agile and informed.

The journey ahead for anyone working with microservices is one of **constant growth** and **experimentation**. Whether you're optimizing existing systems, integrating new technologies, or scaling services to handle increased traffic, remember that the key to success in the microservices space lies in your ability to adapt, experiment, and continually learn from both your successes and challenges.

Embrace the challenges, leverage the power of distributed systems, and always be ready to explore the next big idea in microservices architecture. Your journey in mastering microservices is just beginning, and the possibilities are limitless.

www.ingramcontent.com/pod-product-compliance
Lightning Source LLC
Chambersburg PA
CBHW071237050326
40690CB00011B/2153